THEATER OF WAR

First published in the UK in 2014 by
Intellect, The Mill, Parnall Road, Fishponds, Bristol, BS16 3JG, UK

First published in the USA in 2014 by
Intellect, The University of Chicago Press, 1427 E. 60th Street, Chicago,
IL 60637, USA

A catalogue record for this book is available from the
British Library.

Series editor: Alfredo Cramerotti
Copy-editor: MPS Technologies and Jessica Mitchell
Cover and layout design: Stephanie Sarlos
Cover image: © Meredith Davenport
Production managers: Tim Elameer and Steve Harries

ISBN 978-1-78320-180-8
ePDF ISBN 978-1-78320-415-1

Printed & bound by Gwasg Gomer Cyf / Gomer Press Ltd, UK

THEATER OF WAR

edited by Meredith Davenport

intellect Bristol, UK / Chicago, USA

CONTENTS

RECOUNTING MATTERS
Alfredo Cramerotti

In 1889 Lewis Carroll published *Sylvie and Bruno*, in which a "proto-nerd" character called "Mein Herr" explains the pitfalls of creating too precise a map

> Mein Herr: "What do you consider the largest map that would be really useful?"
> Sylvie: "About six inches to the mile."
>
> "Only six inches!" exclaimed Mein Herr. "We very soon got to six yards to the mile. Then we tried a hundred yards to the mile. And then came the grandest idea of all! We actually made a map of the country, on the scale of a mile to the mile!"
>
> "Have you used it much?" I enquired.
>
> "It has never been spread out, yet," said Mein Herr: "the farmers objected: they said it would cover the whole country, and shut out the sunlight! So we use the country itself, as its own map, and I assure you it does nearly as well."[1]

In reality, too, techniques of representation have gone through innumerable "improvements," as attempts at precision continue to produce progressive information and communication tools. The momentum of modernity requires that we track history from the closest possible observation point, preferably with the observer in the middle of the event itself, reporting its unfolding in real-time. As a matter of fact, this closeness often "blocks out the sun" as we come to lack any critical distance on the matters reported, and we end up taking for "real" what effectively is a blurred compilation of fragments.

In contrast to an idea of history that celebrates either its media of communication (in modern times) or the absence of historical forms of representation (where there are few and far images or written records), a theatrical approach to recounting history "compresses" time. Theater can be a tool to comprehend reality through re-enactments of specific moments, in particular places; it gives life to past, present, or future events by scripting them. Re-enactment has already been massively mediatized (sourcing its material from media or personal narratives), but it does not, in this sense, provide a spurious image of the event, since it leaves open to the viewer the possibility to go back to the original narrative and "de-compress" the story.

Instead of an archaeological space (or time) reconstruction, the re-enactment embeds a desire of repeating *ad infinitum* the map of the territory. The event or the story re-enactment follows is already "closed", since it has already happened, so it allows its re-opening for further individual and collective speculation, in which each repetition is as significant as it is different. •

ENDNOTES
1   My thanks to Peter Nowogrodzki for pointing out this passage in his text "On Exactitude in Science," in Alfredo Cramerotti (ed.), *The Blind*, Bristol, UK: Intellect.

IN PURSUIT OF WAR
Fred Ritchin

War is known for a sense of purpose, for its timely acts of heroism, for the focus of its armed participants and the bonding among them. War is known for its horrific casualties, its dubious victories, its loose relationship to the truth and its landscapes of ruin. War is also known for its glamour. Tim Page, a photographer who rode around on his motorbike during the Vietnam War, where he would be terribly wounded, was asked to write a book that would finally take the glamour out of war. His response: "Jesus! . . . Take the glamour out of war! How the hell can you do that? You can't take the glamour out of a tank burning or a helicopter blowing up. It's like trying to take the glamour out of sex. War is good for you."[1]

Some of the actors in Meredith Davenport's *Theater of War* seem far removed from war's glamour, even a bit unsure of themselves in their stateside roles. Distant from the scenes of battle, seeking to re-create and explore war's legacies on an altogether different landscape, they come across as hesitant time travelers hoping, perhaps, that the costumes they wear and the rituals they embrace will provide meaning—or at least connection—in ways that the secular, outside world cannot. Without the trauma of blood-letting, they appear to be trying to create a stage in which tradition, and even honor, can still command applause.

Where do they get their inspiration? From family members and friends and, in part, through media, dependent upon its depictions to replicate history's battles. What did they wear? How did they stand? What were the weapons? In which ways did they move? But they seem attracted, as well, to an era before media became triumphant—the camera displacing time and space, television encouraging a particular kind of passivity, and now the multi-player online games with competing avatars shooting to kill. Vulnerable to the elements, extricating themselves from a life of chain stores and personal responsibilities, these actors seem to keep one foot in another time—as if, after being photographed by Meredith Davenport, they would have few qualms about posing for Roger Fenton or another nineteenth-century photographer with a bulky view camera.

Or perhaps, in Davenport's pictures, the two centuries of now and then entwine more than usually happens: time slows, events have duration, bodies have presence, and spaces remain open and unsettled. In this case, both photographer and subjects seem intent on decelerating the rhythm of conflict (or its approximation) to try and engage with some of war's substance and strategies. Although the questions may never be articulated so directly, they seem liminal: Why would one want to shoot another being? What does it mean to win in war? Why does war seem, at times, to be much like a children's game?

Rather than war's greatest hits—the stuff of contemporary magazines—we find ourselves on its backlot, waiting for the casting director while meeting those investigating its premises and its pageantry. War is theatrical, and its spectacle is the fodder for movies and photographs; its script comes in many versions.

Just a few years after their medium's invention, photographers went in search of war, drawn to the fields of battle in horse-drawn wagons with portable darkrooms and tripod-mounted cameras. Given the limited technology of the mid-nineteenth century there was no way to record the fast-moving battle, so photographers such as Fenton, Felice Beato, Matthew Brady, Alexander Gardner, and others, had to use their imagination to transmit the import of what had already happened, framing the conflict's aftermath in their viewfinder. It is not surprising then that some photographers would at times re-arrange the scene, moving cannon balls or bones or rifles to make a more dramatic image.

Davenport's photographs are also about aftermaths—war as re-imagined, as memory incarnated. These aftermaths may be years or even decades after the actual events as well as thousands of miles away, appropriated from different cultures and geographies. Her pictures then ask what is the motivation for this re-appropriation, and what are its links to the state of American culture today? Her interest appears to be less in the drama of history, and more in the shifting mores of contemporary society in which the historical is expressed.

We live in a time when war is often covered by photographers forced to "embed" with the troops, contractually constrained from publishing certain kinds of imagery. We also grow more dependent on citizen journalists sending photos and videos of war from their mobile phones, often as participants in the conflict; for example, the most important photographs from the recent US involvement in the war in Iraq were made by soldiers at Abu Ghraib prison, not by professional photojournalists. There are also few if any iconic photographs that have emerged from Afghanistan to help broadly define for the public the longest war in American history.

Sometimes in the ripple of events, rather than in the events themselves—particularly if their depictions are standardized and turned into spectacle—certain truths can emerge. Davenport's images begin to question some of what war is about by dwelling in the realm of make-believe. Given media's repetitive fantasies, in some ways her approach may be, paradoxically, more real. •

NOTES

1   Tim Page, quoted in Harold Evans, "Reporting in the Time of Conflict," Newseum War Stories, n.d. http://www.newseum.org/warstories/essay/romance.htm.

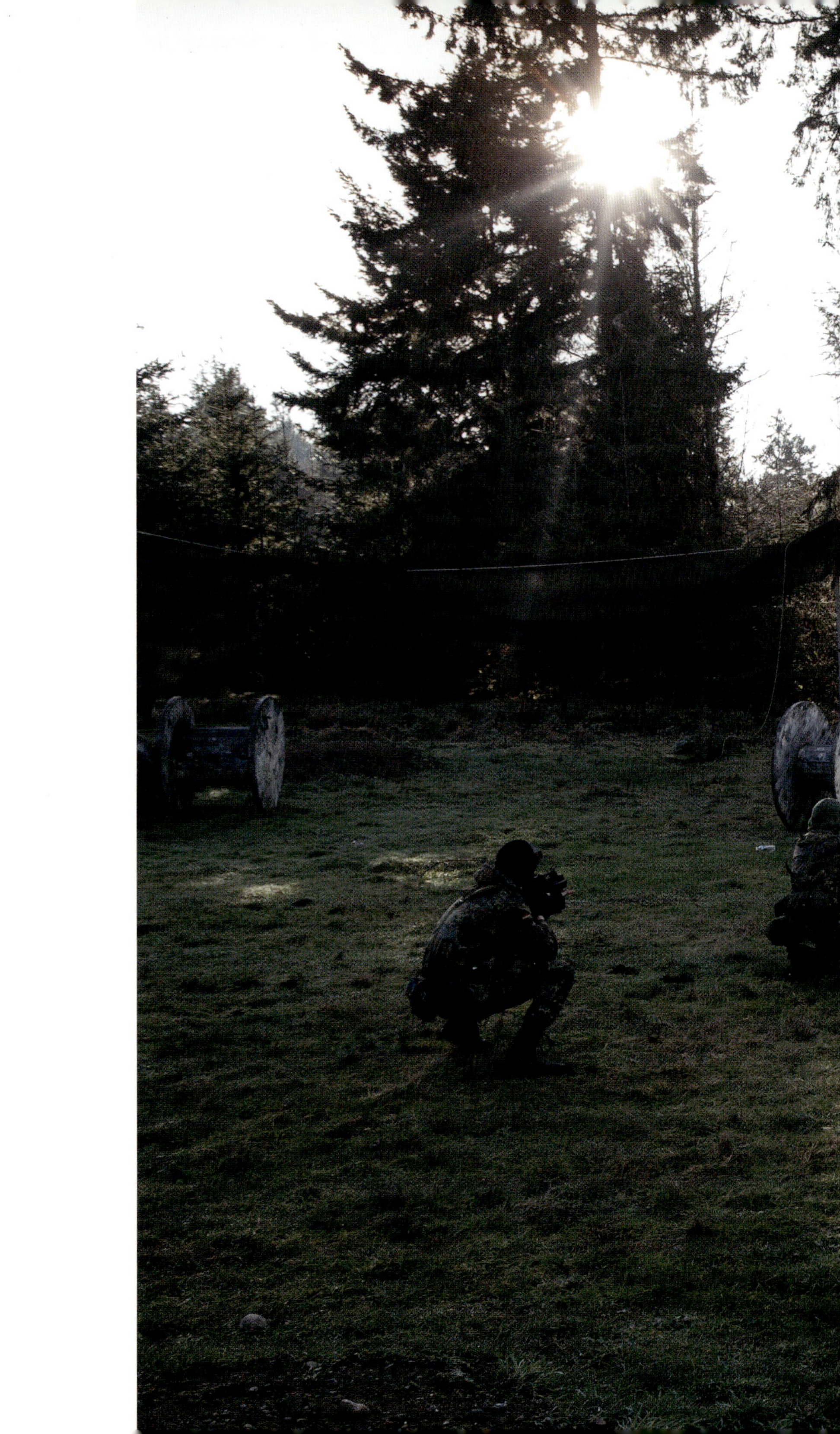

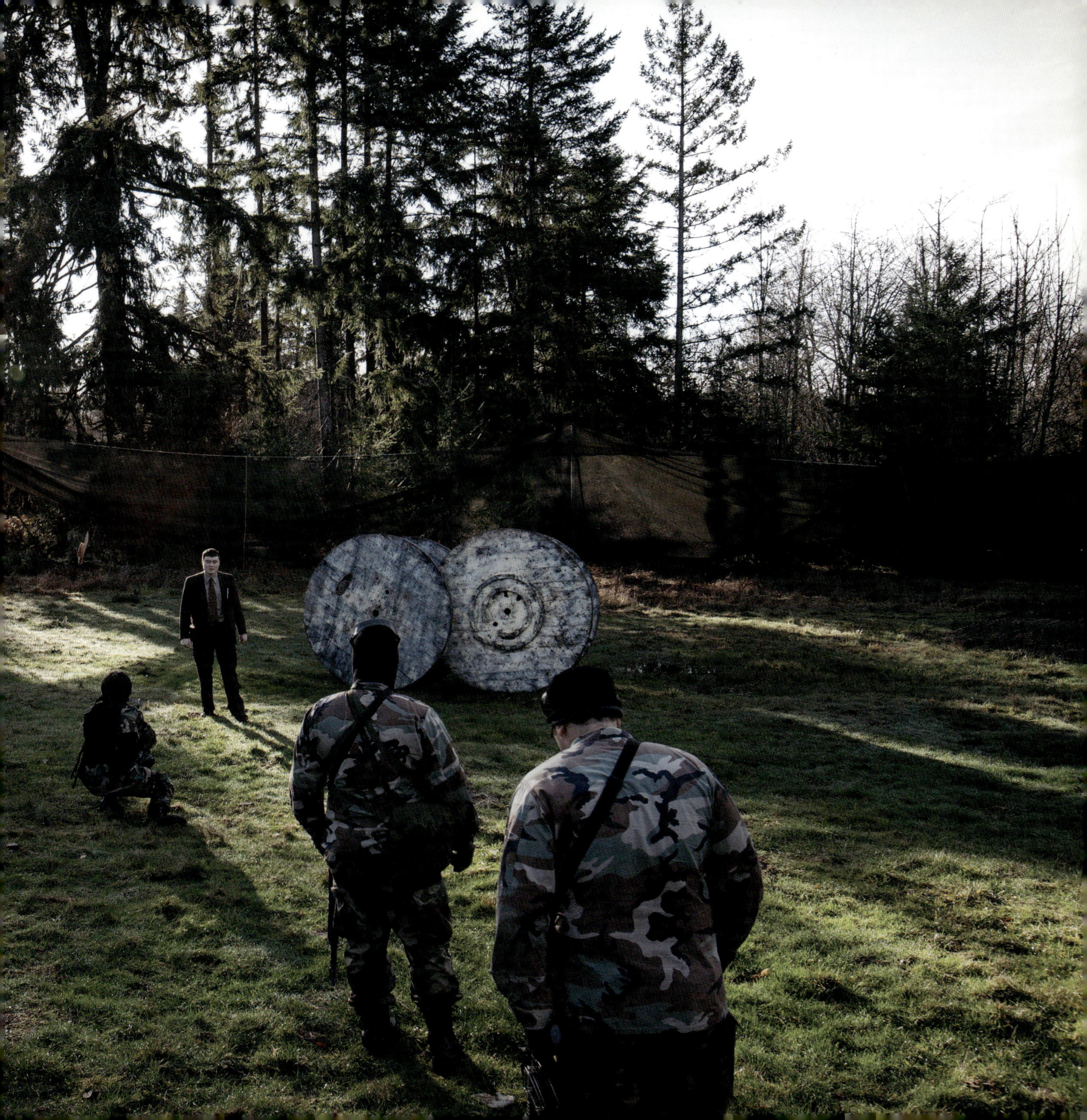

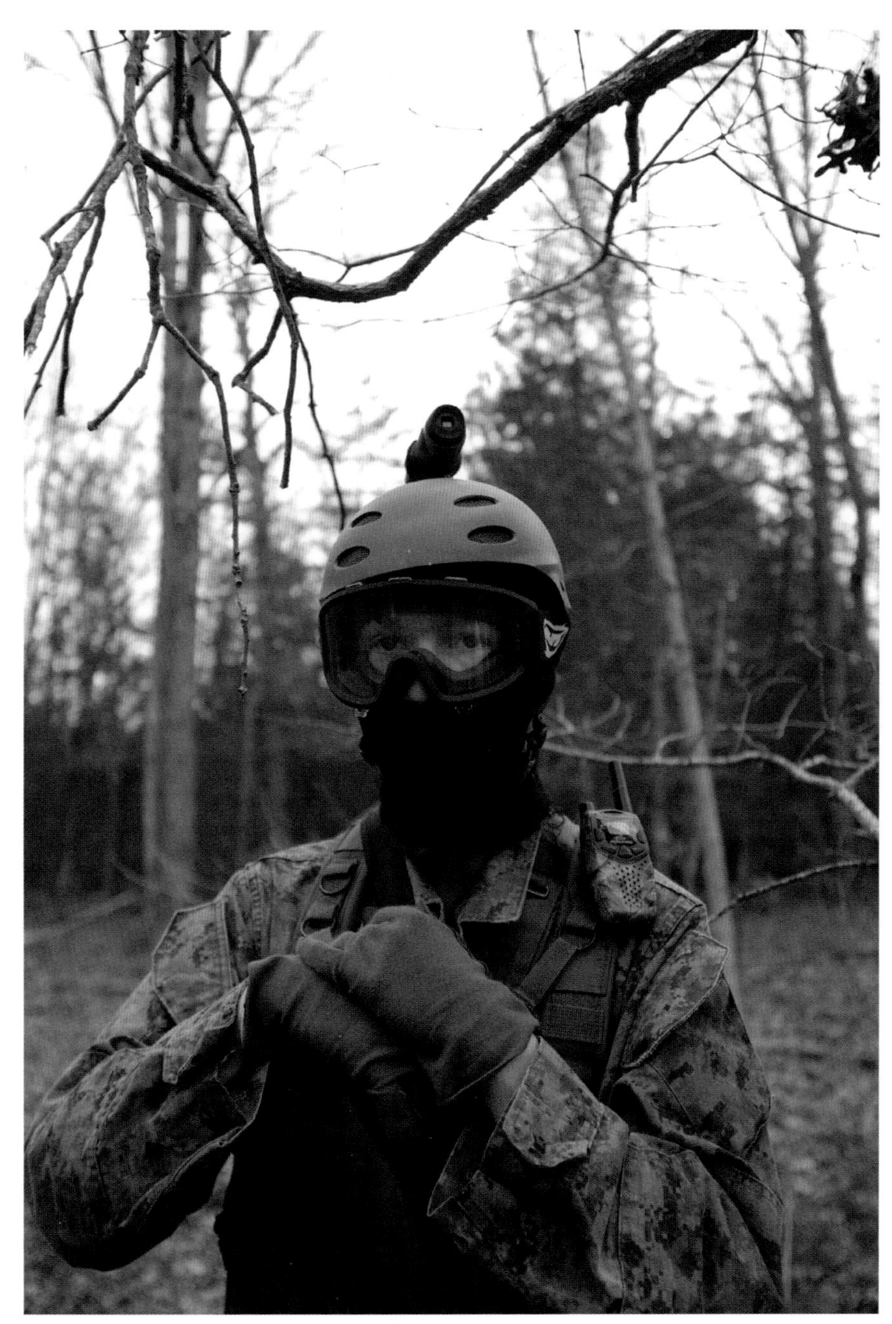

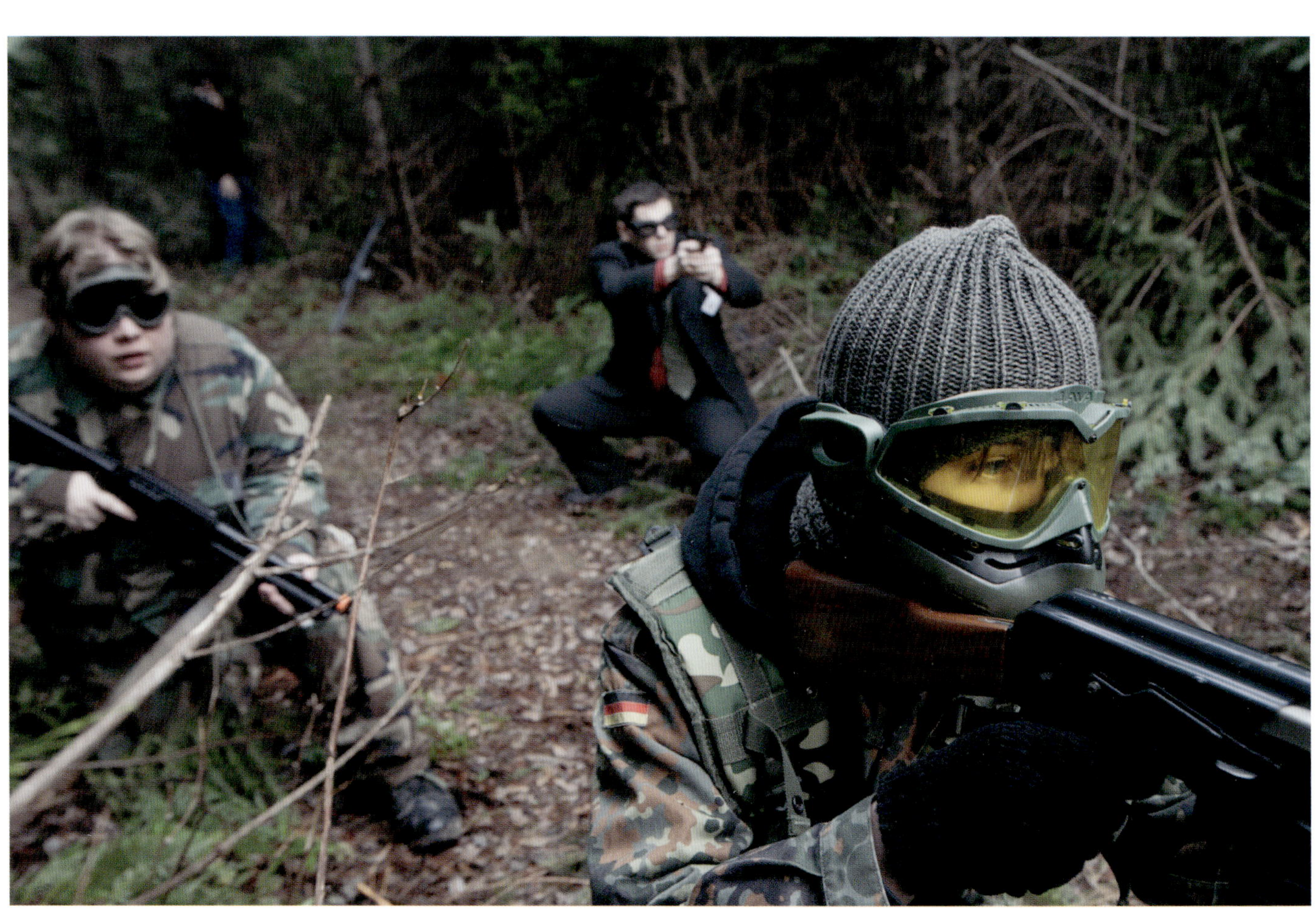

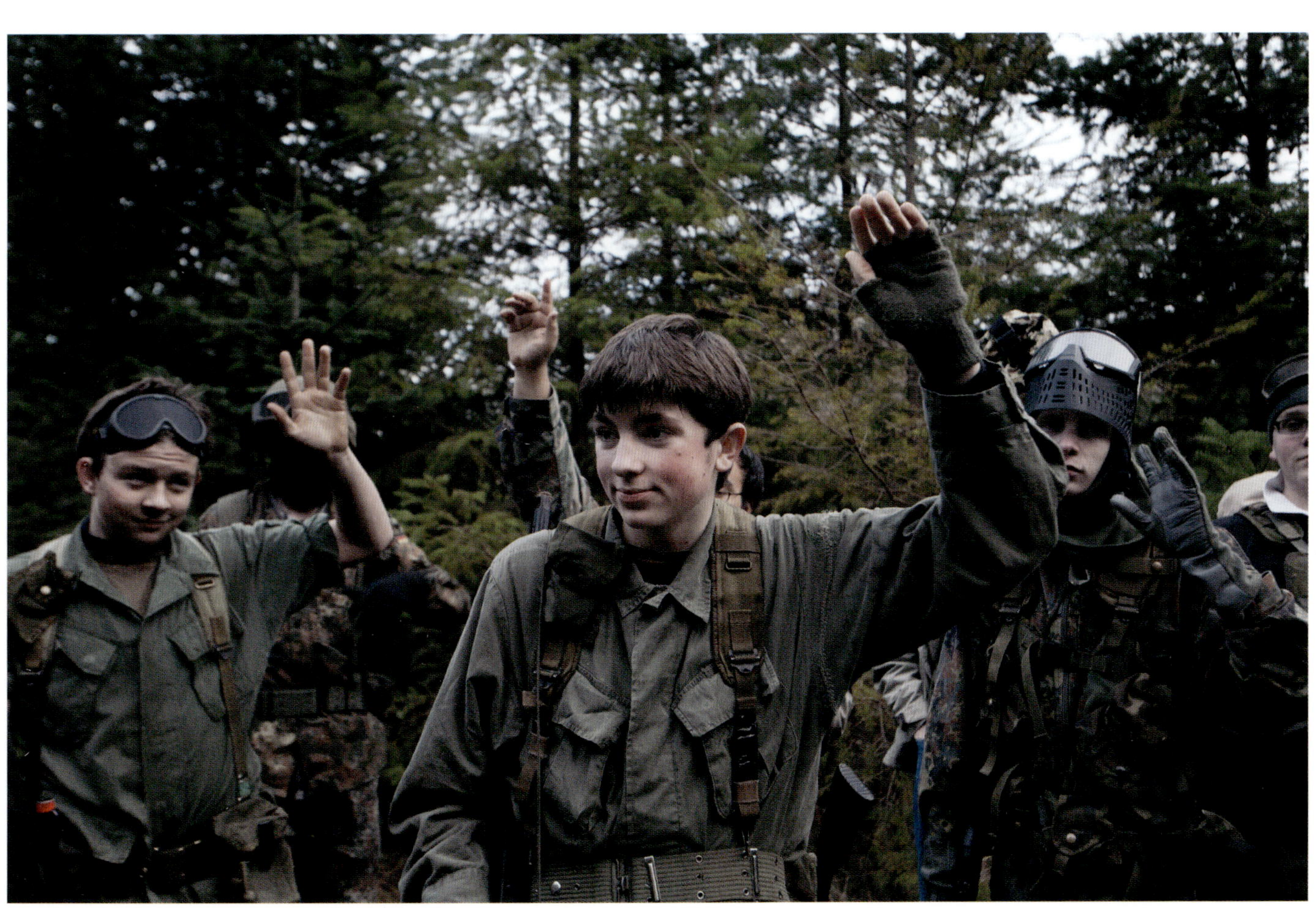

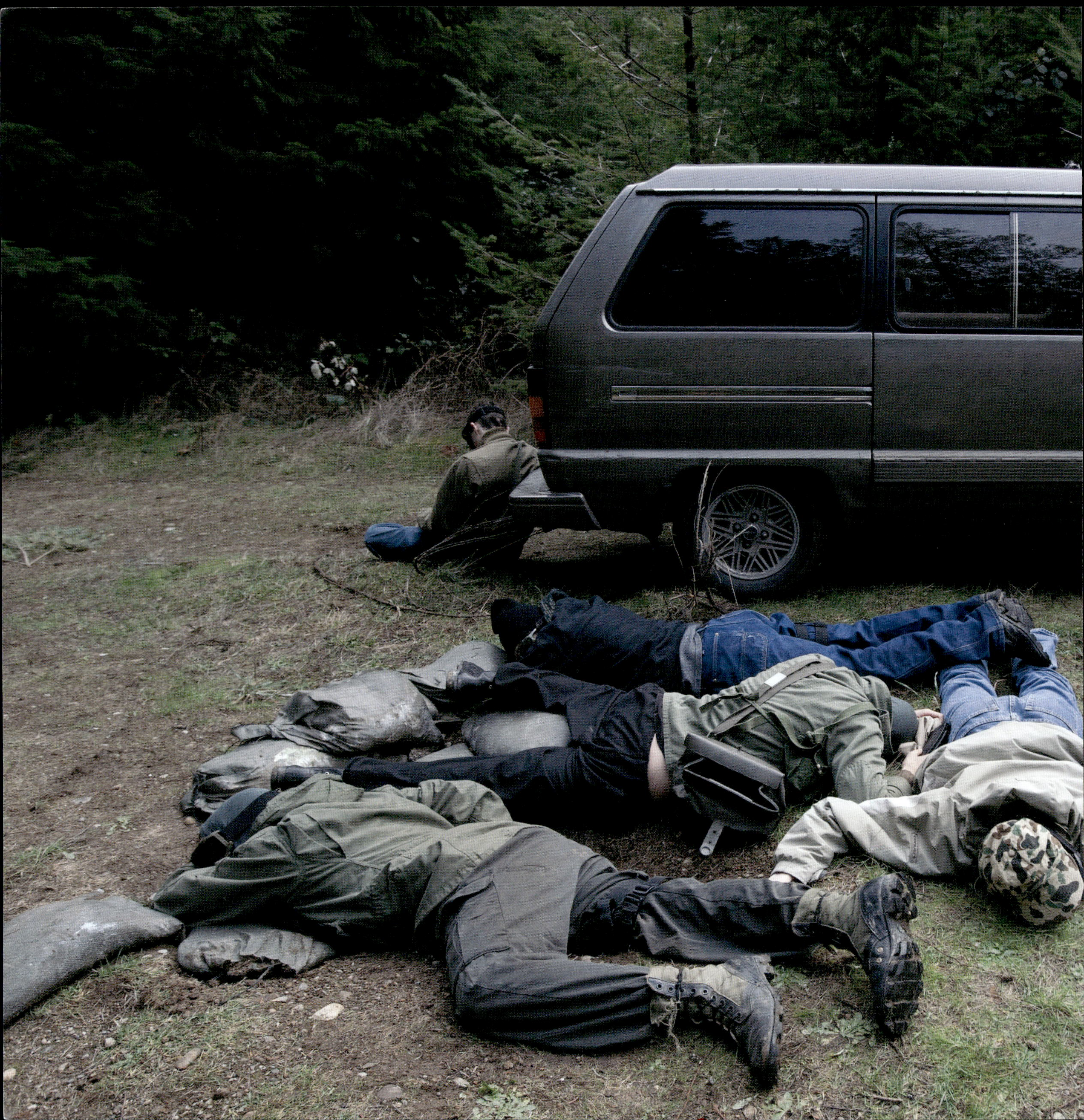

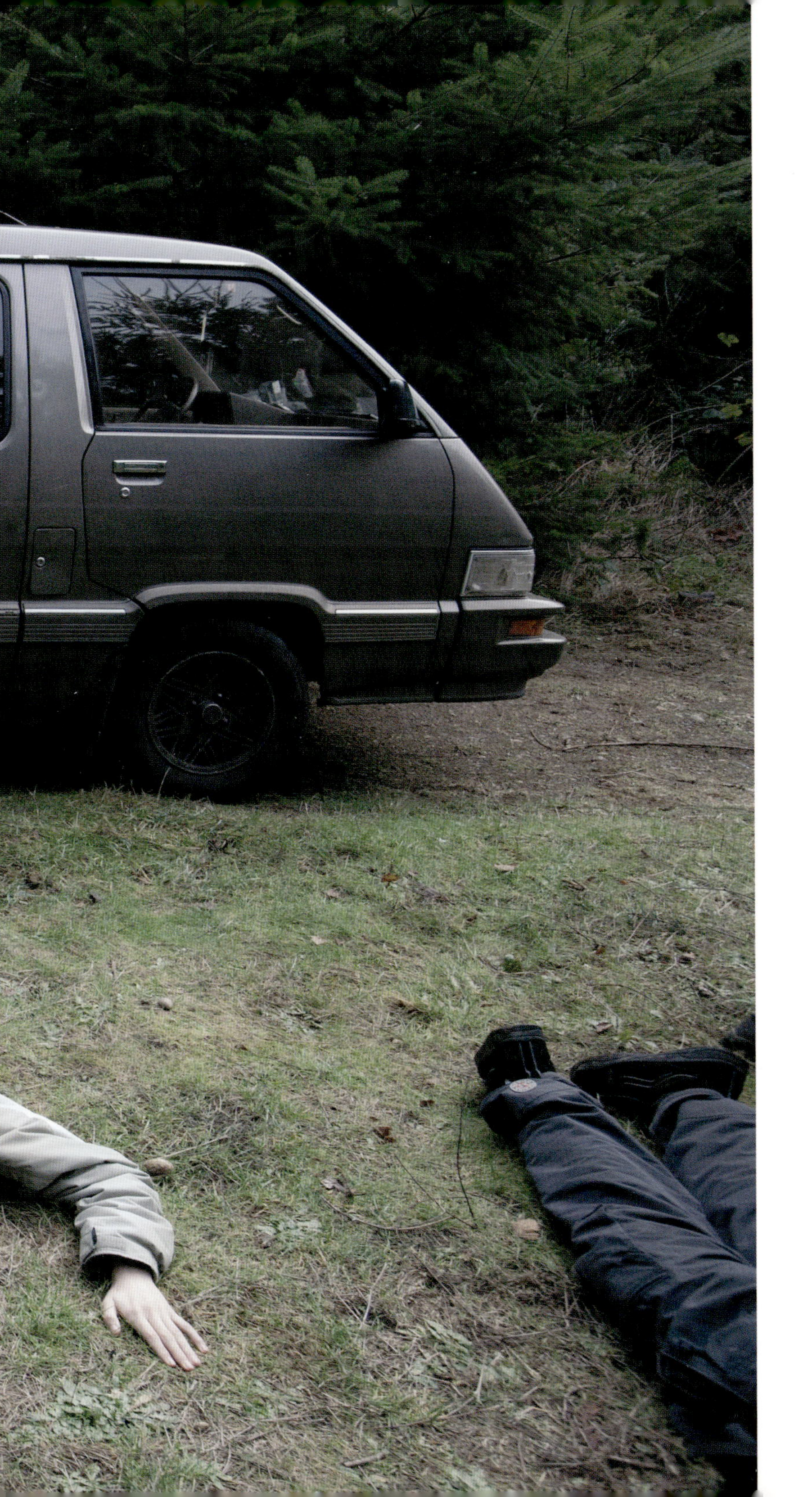

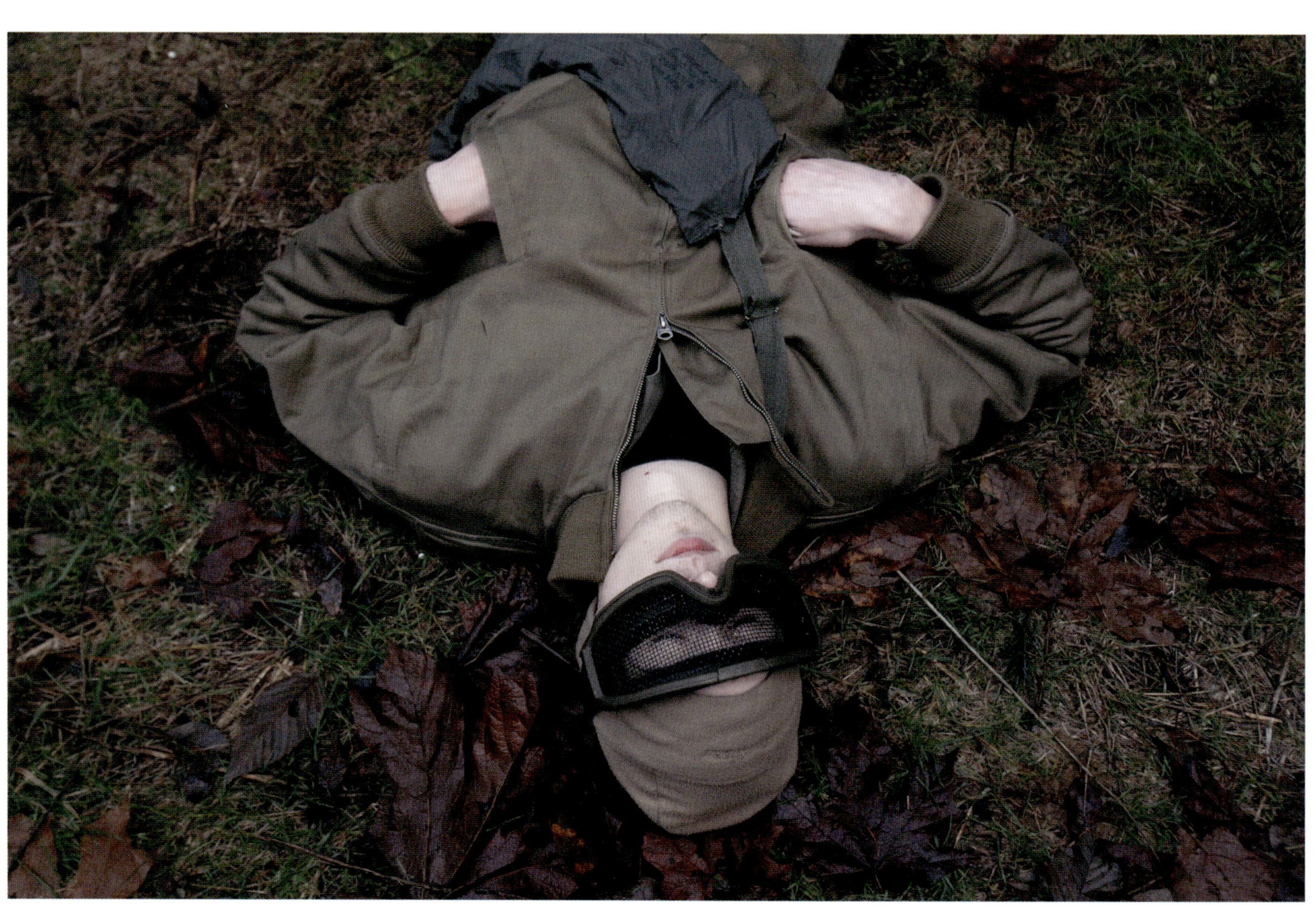

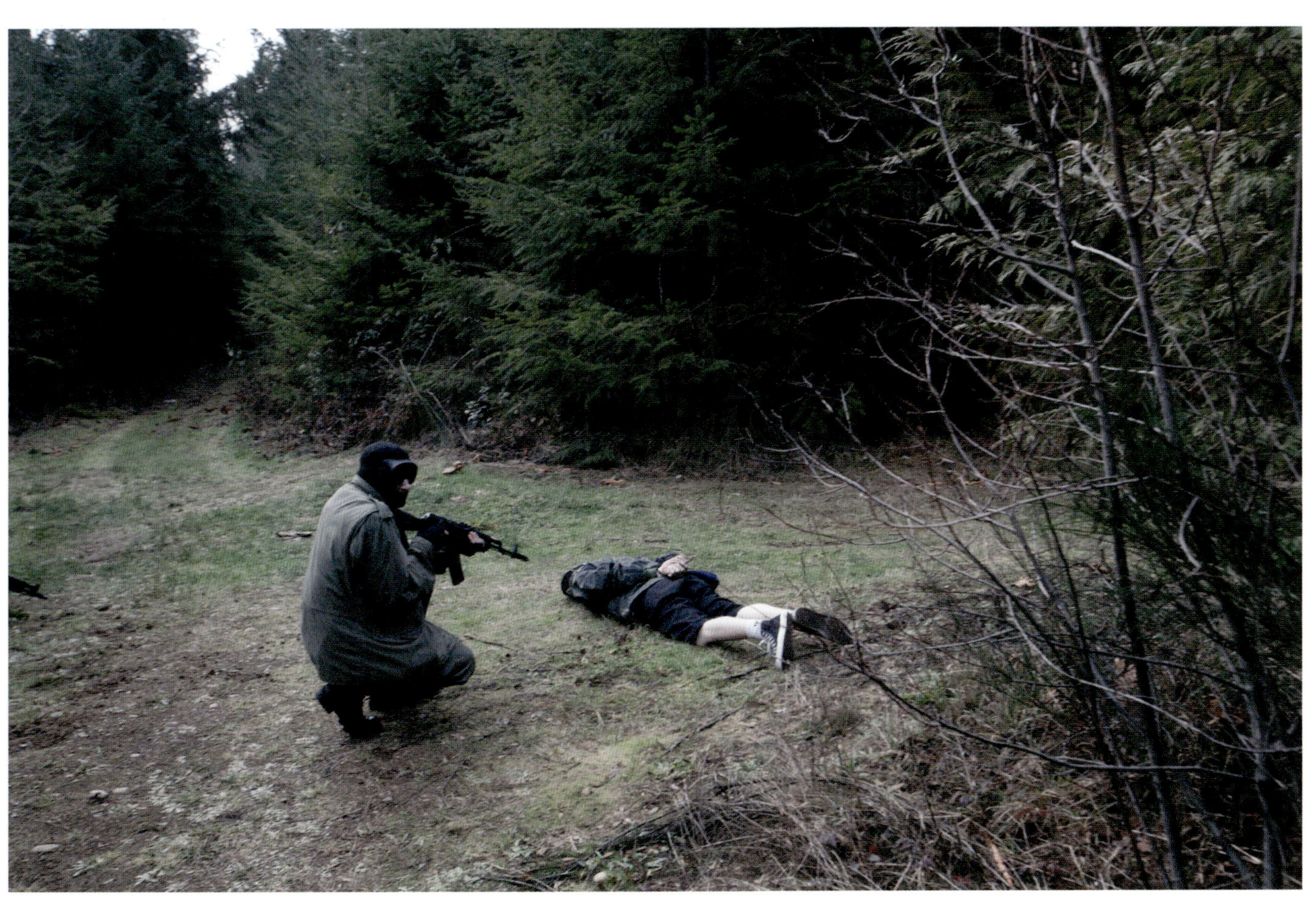

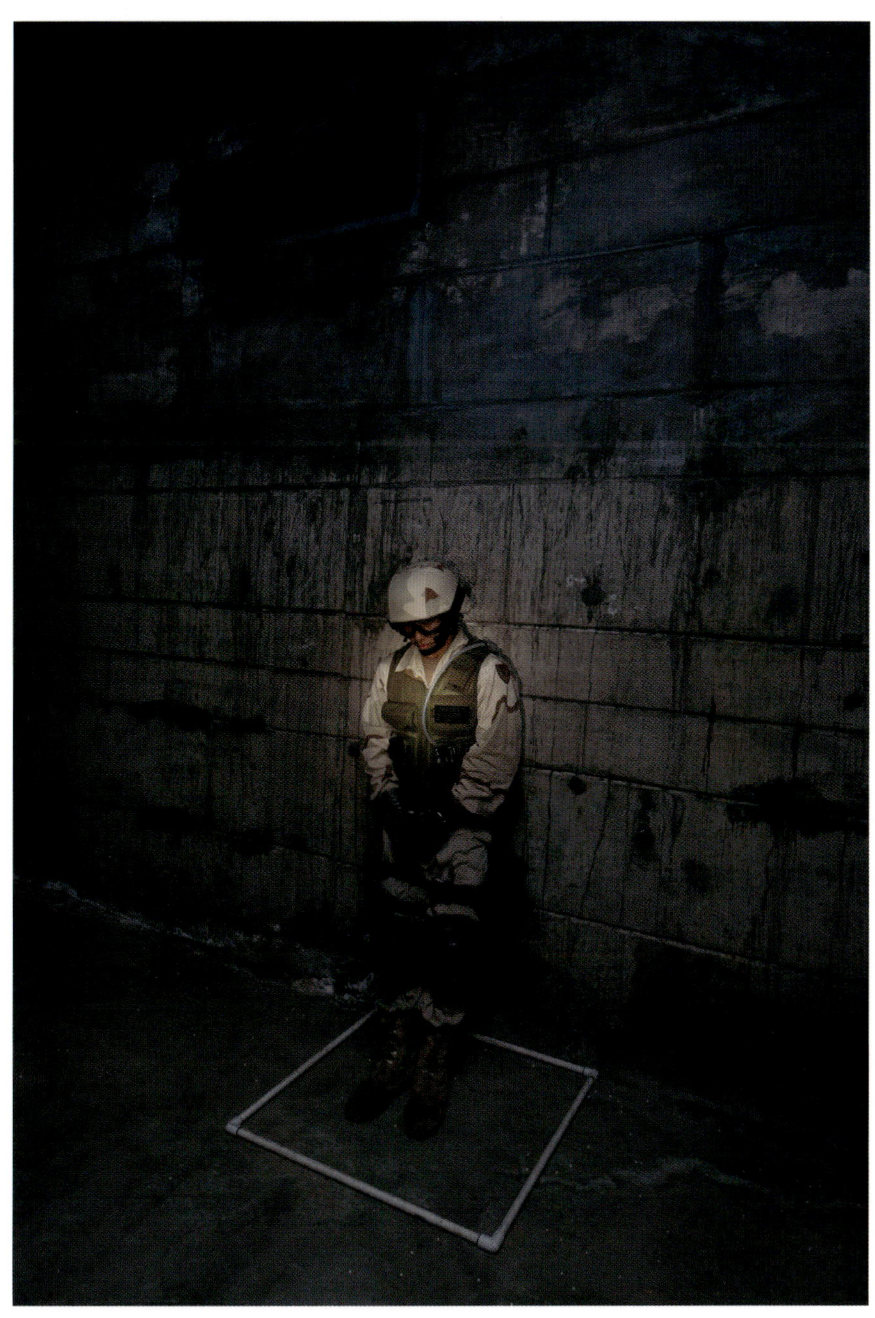

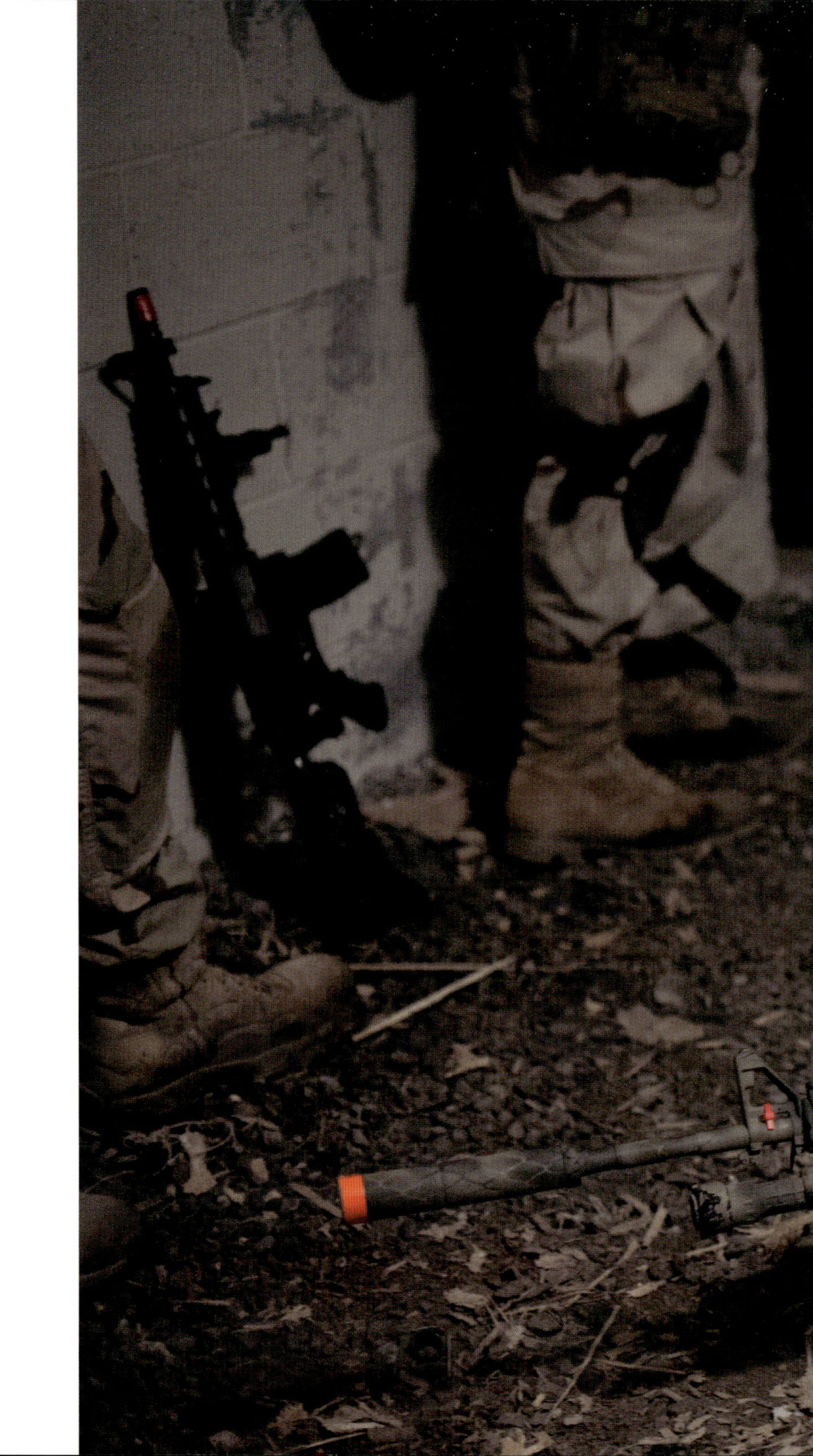

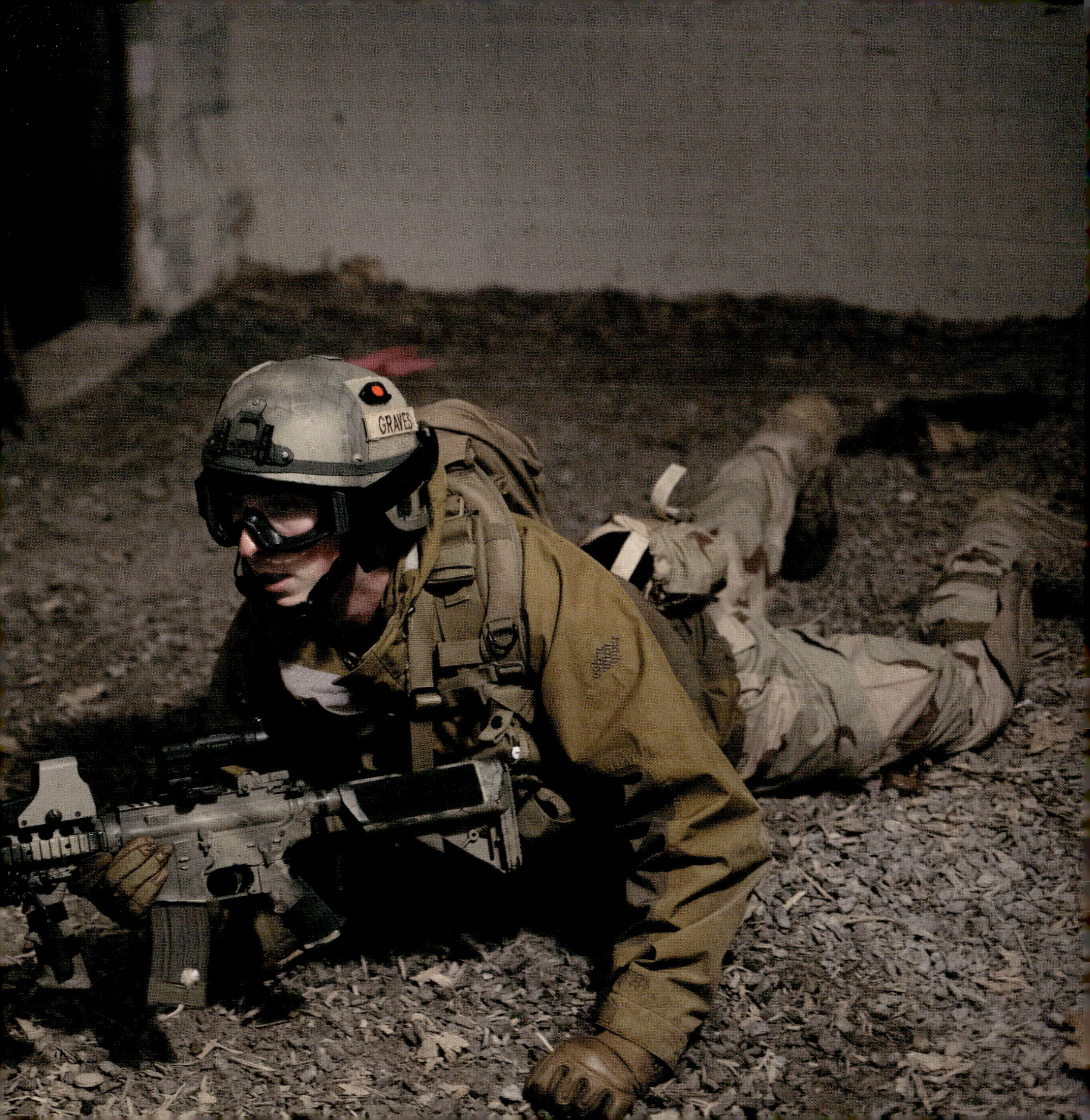

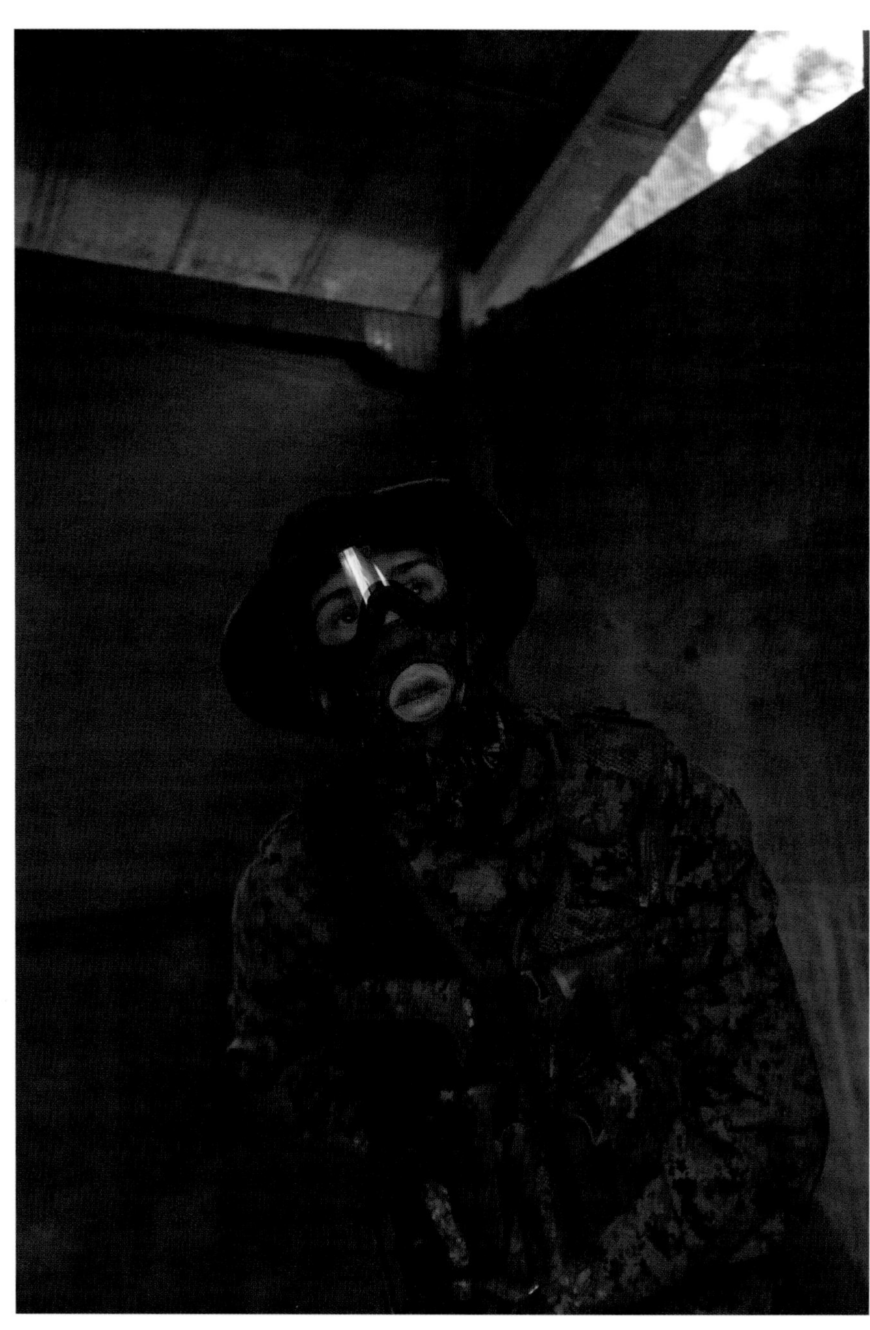

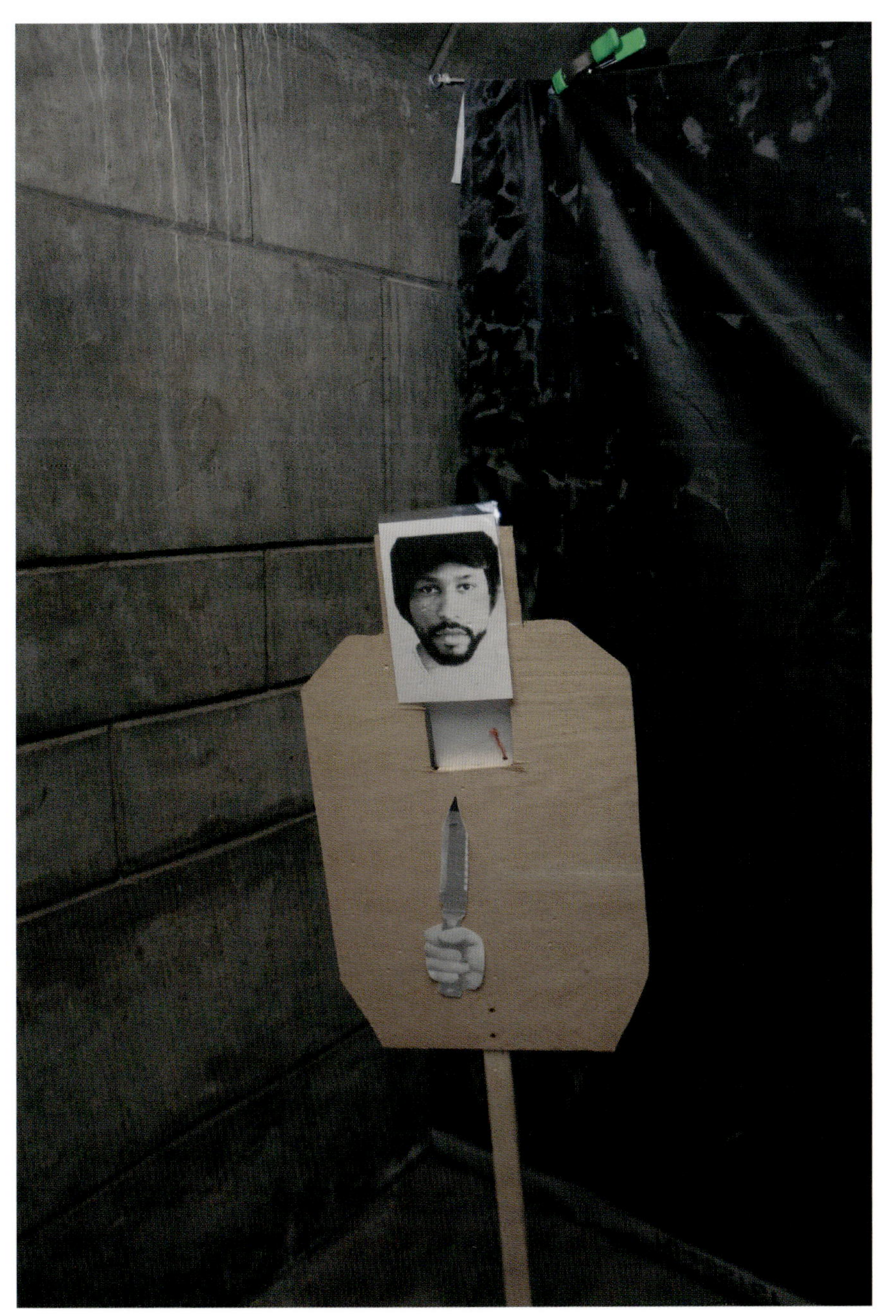

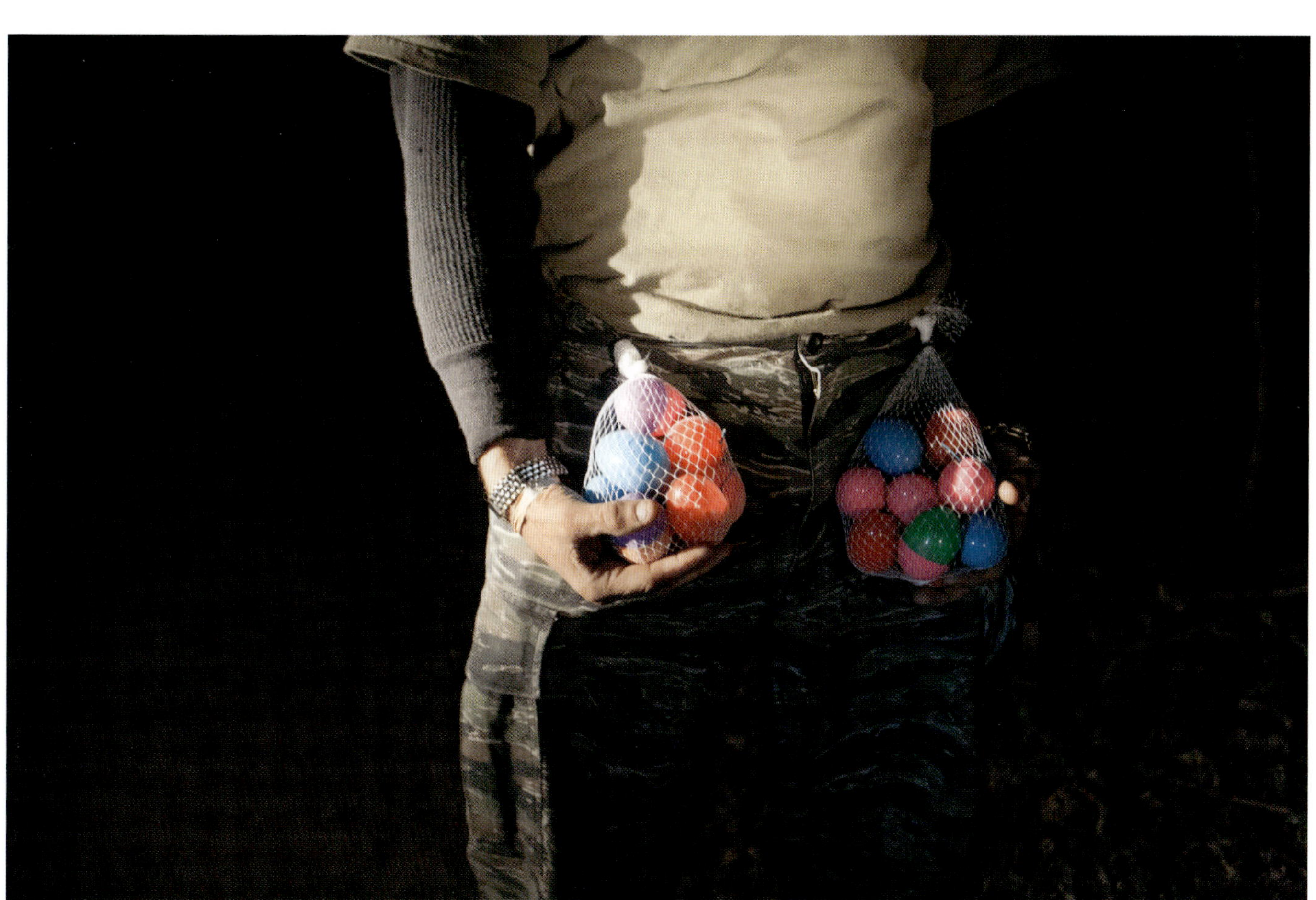

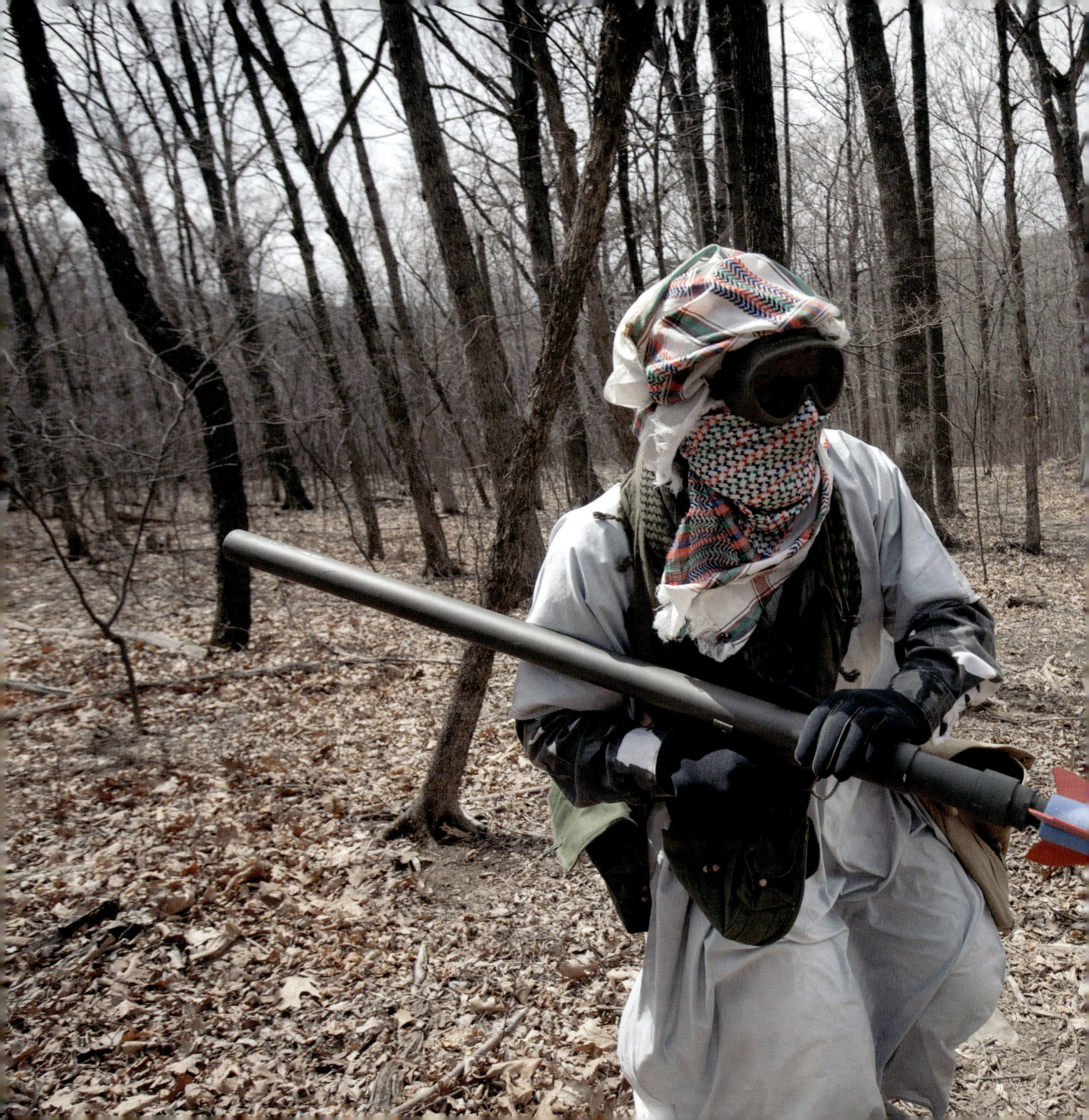

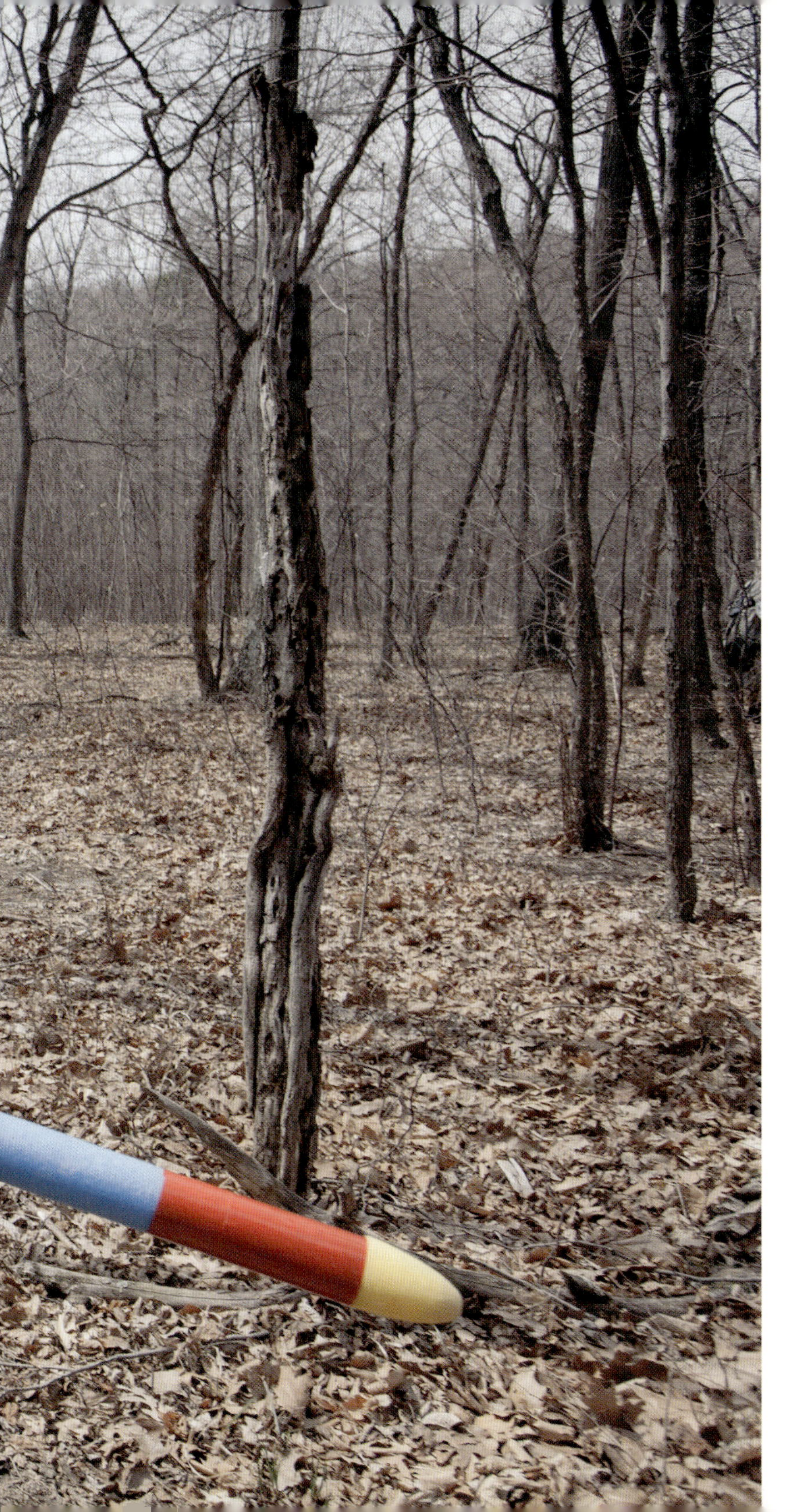

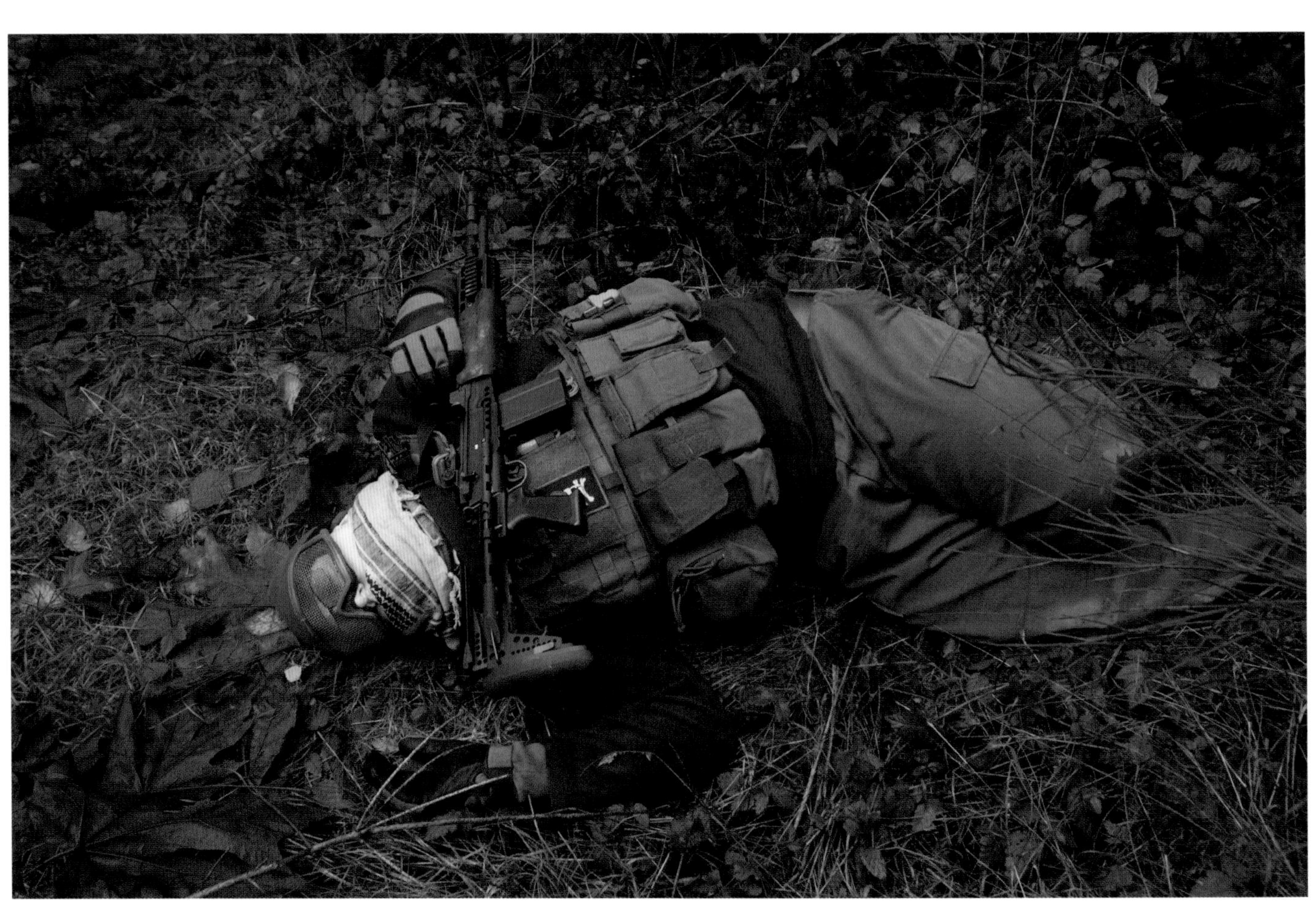

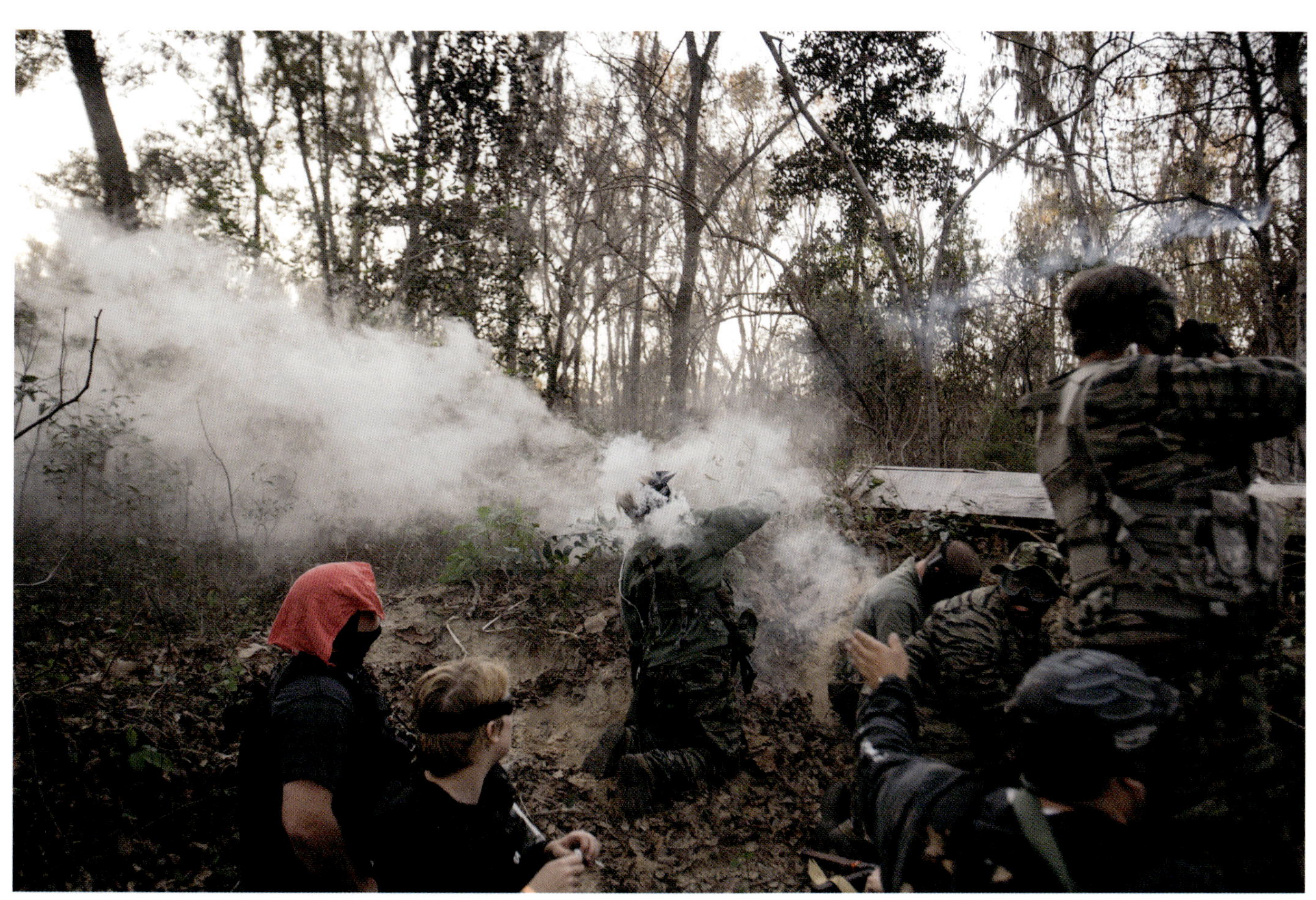

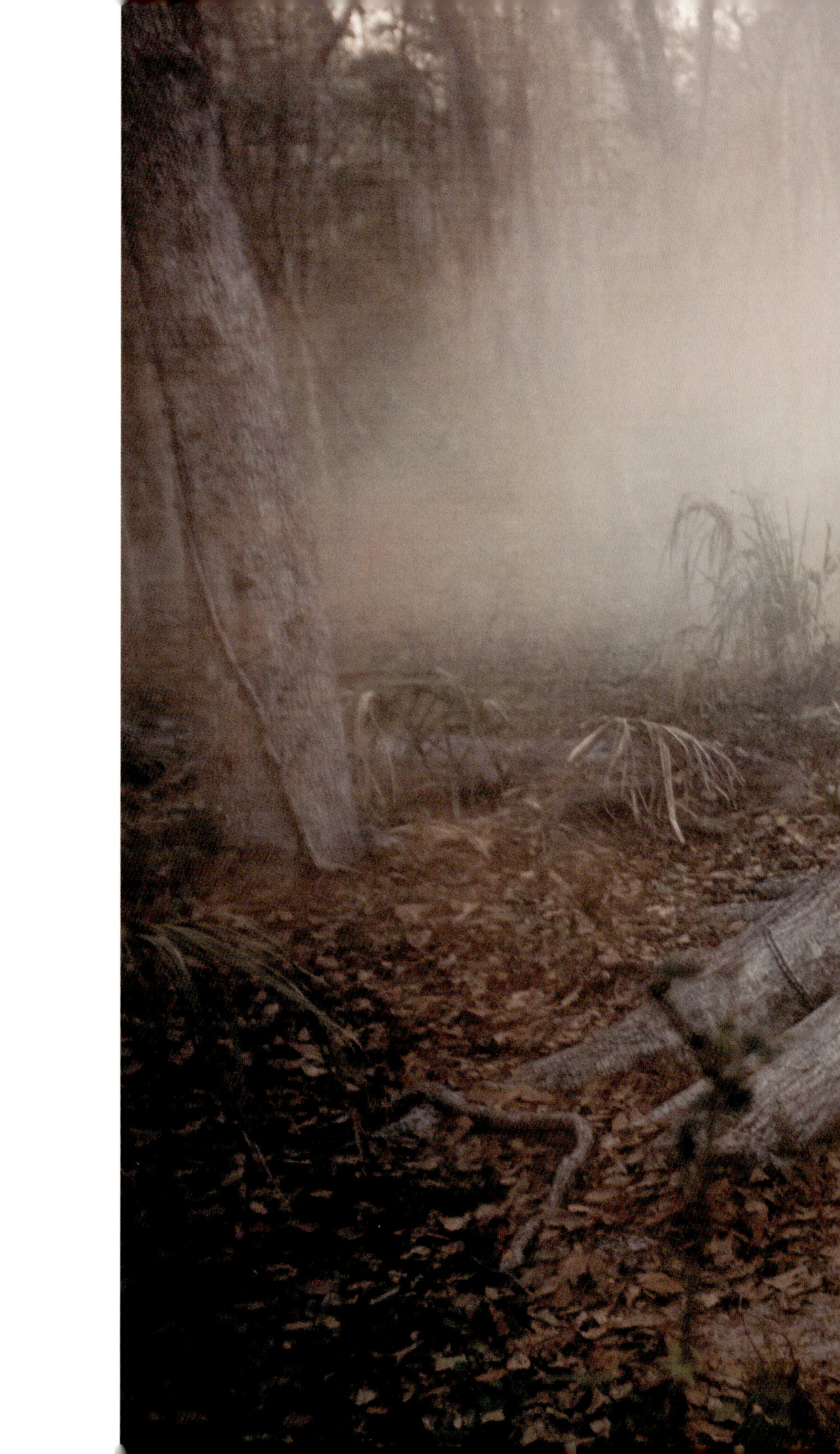

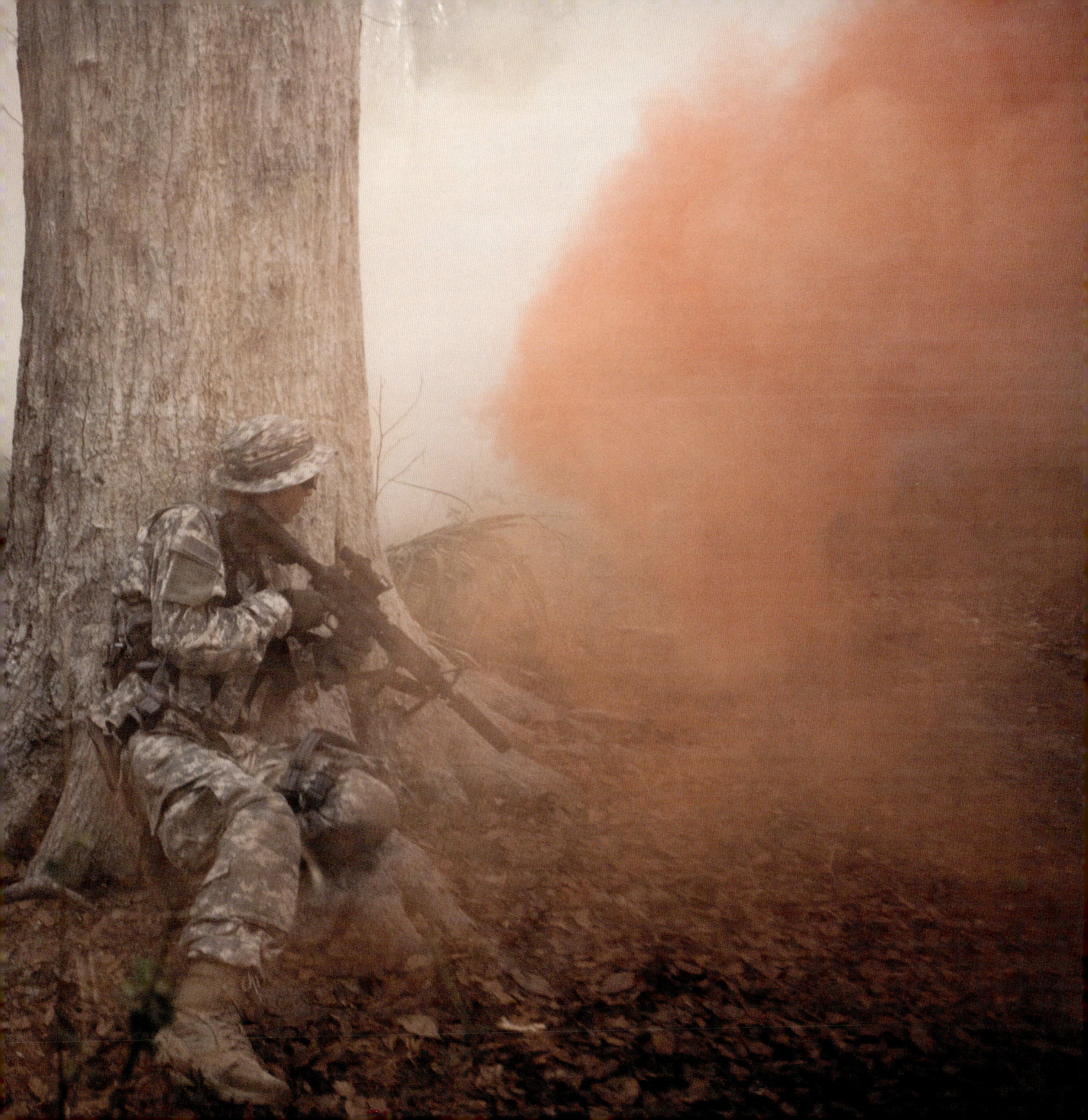

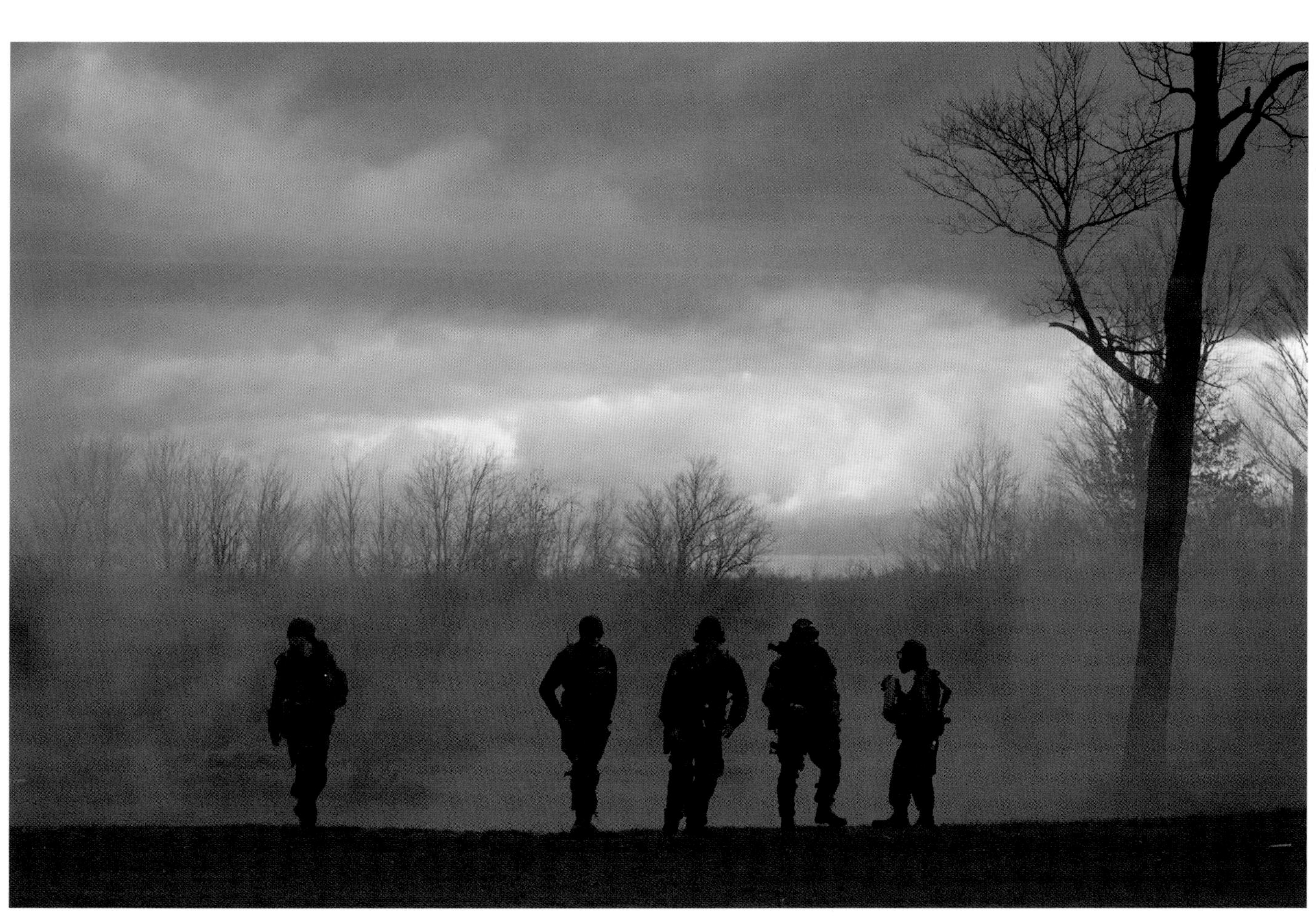

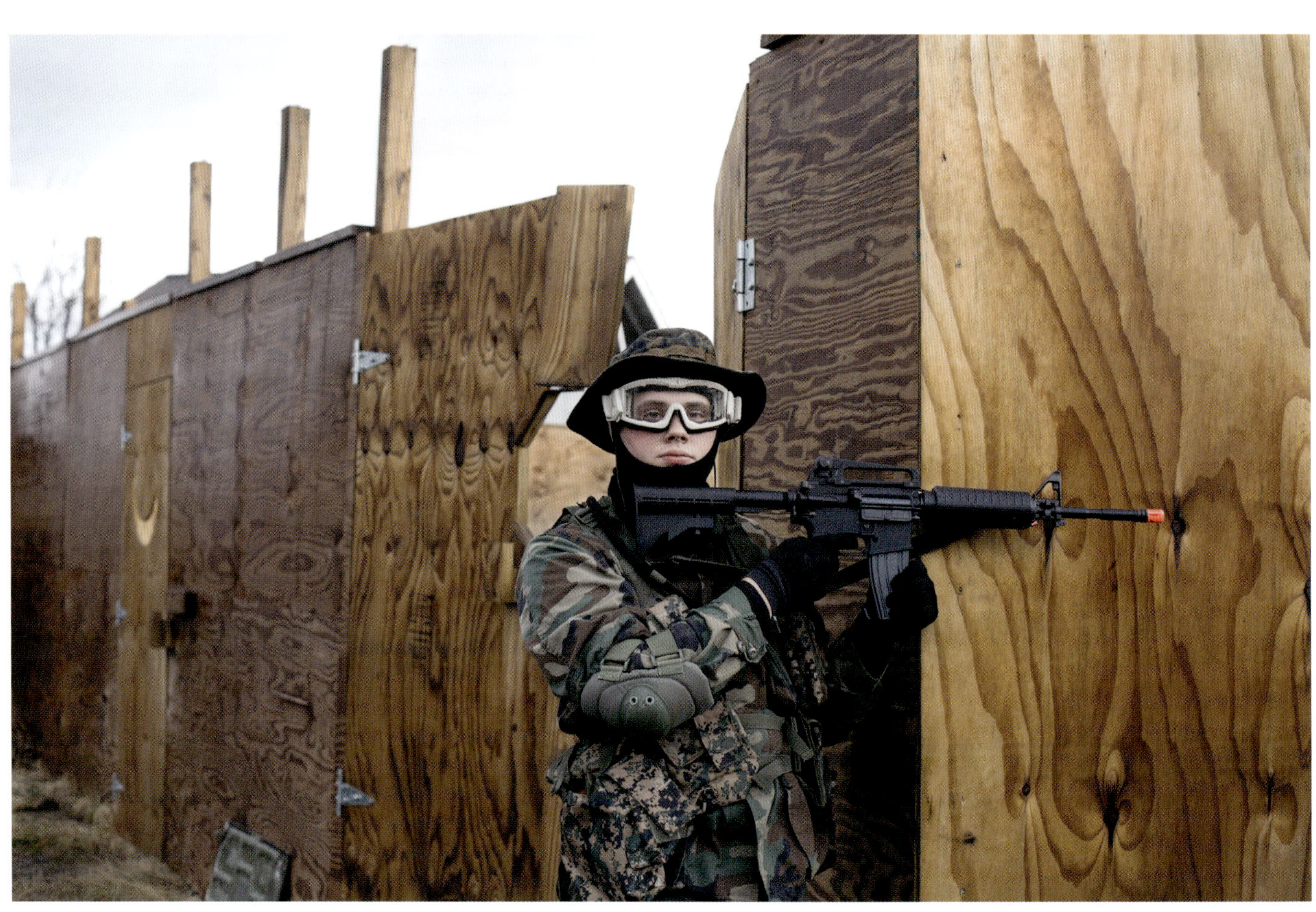

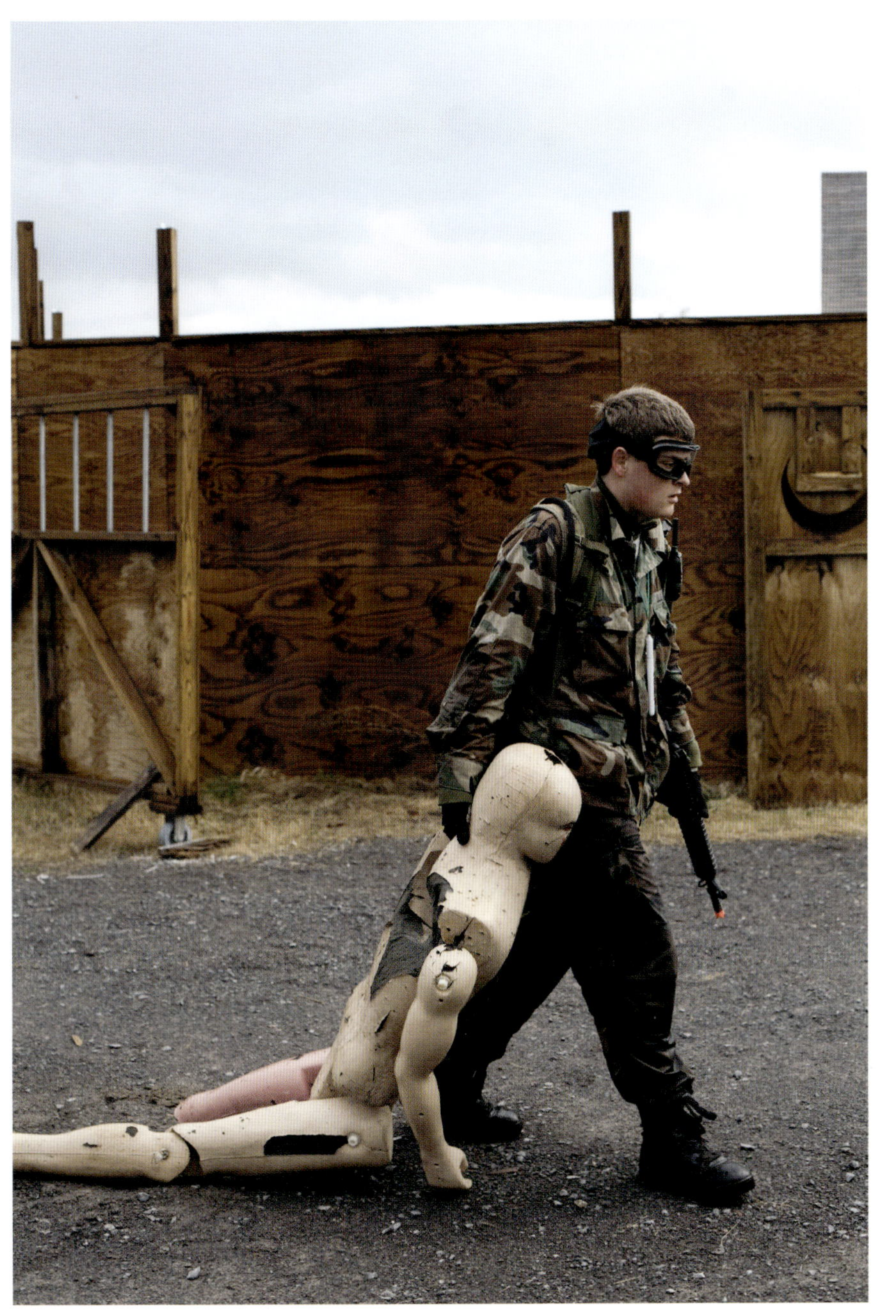

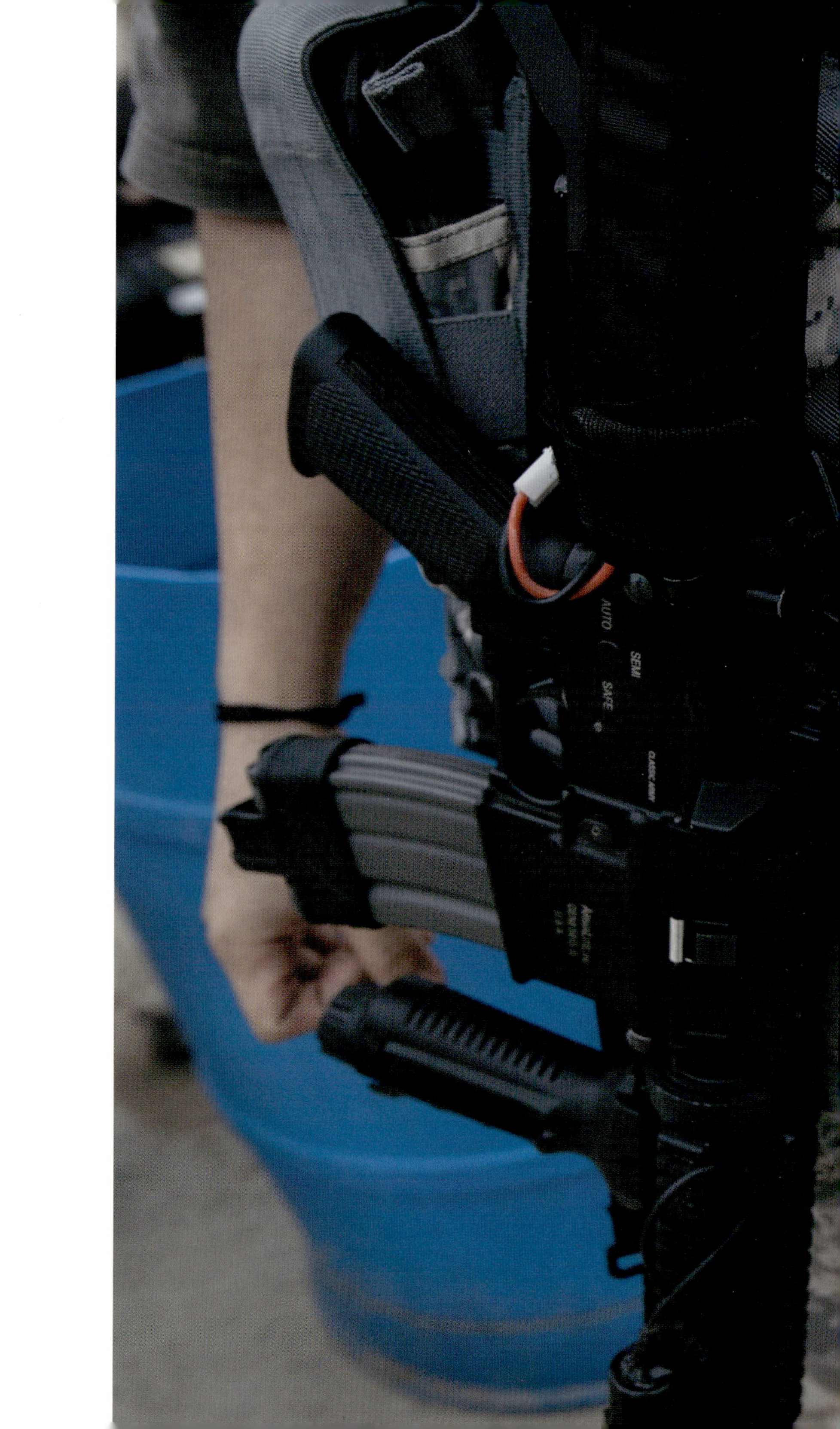

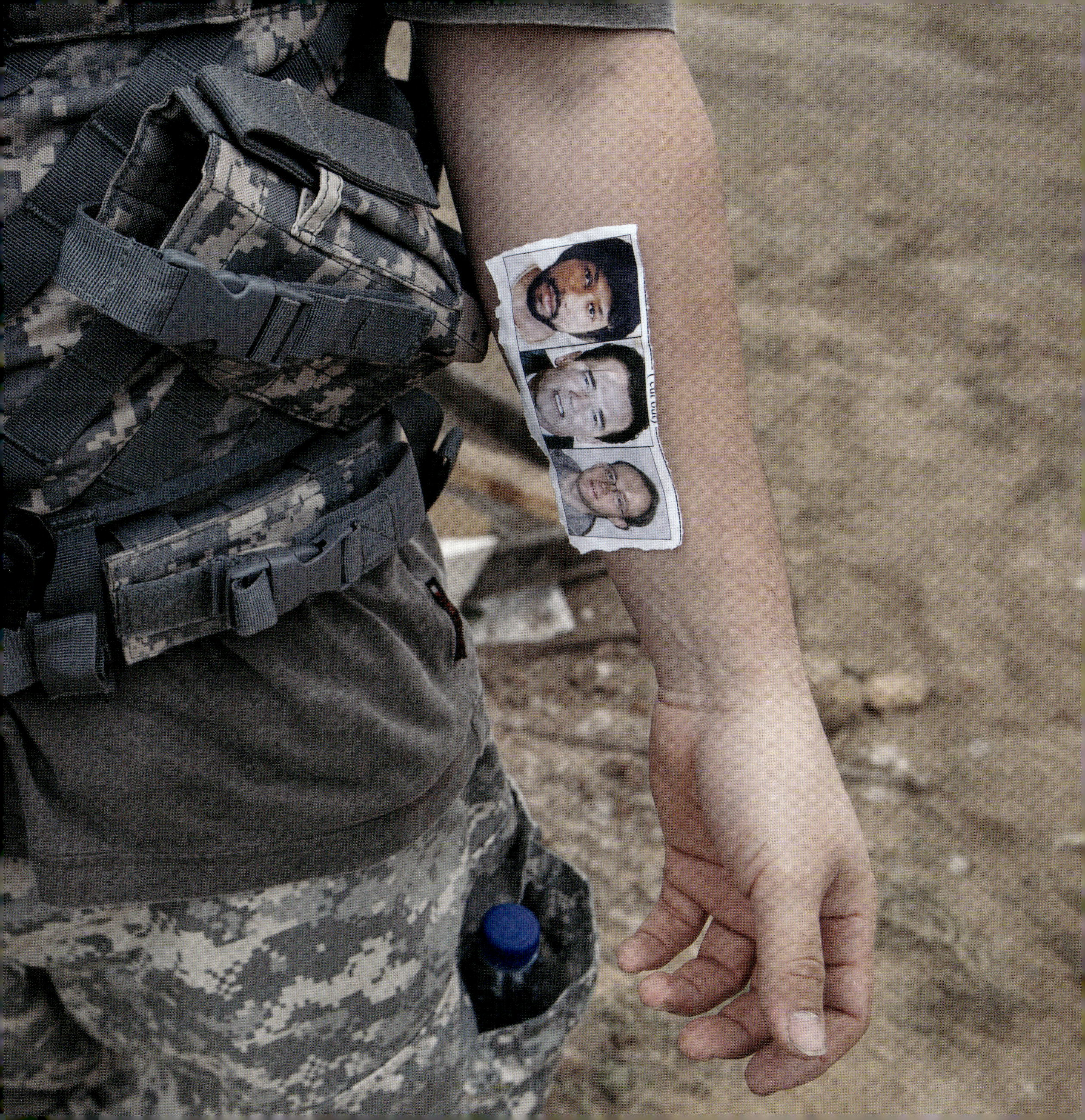

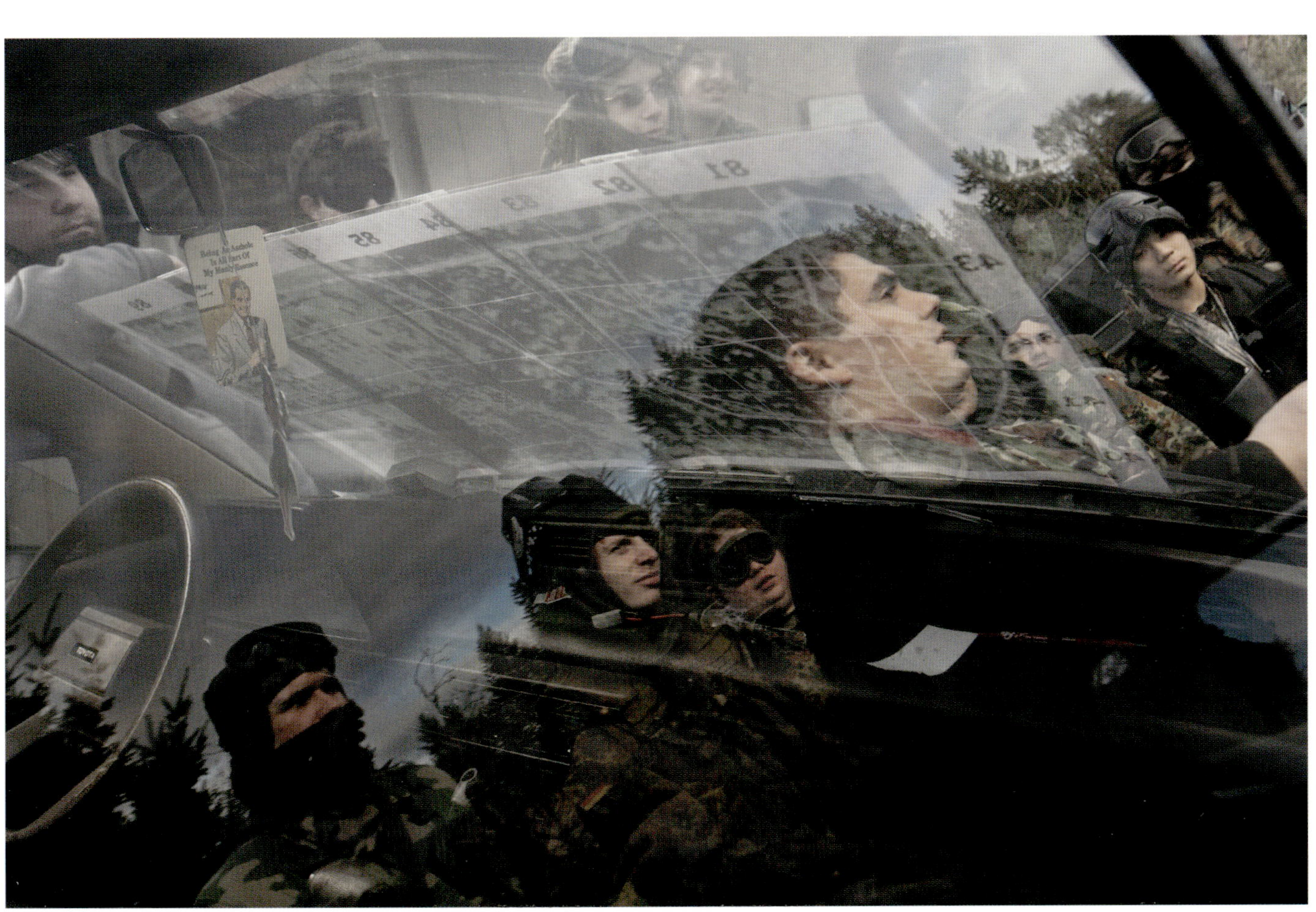

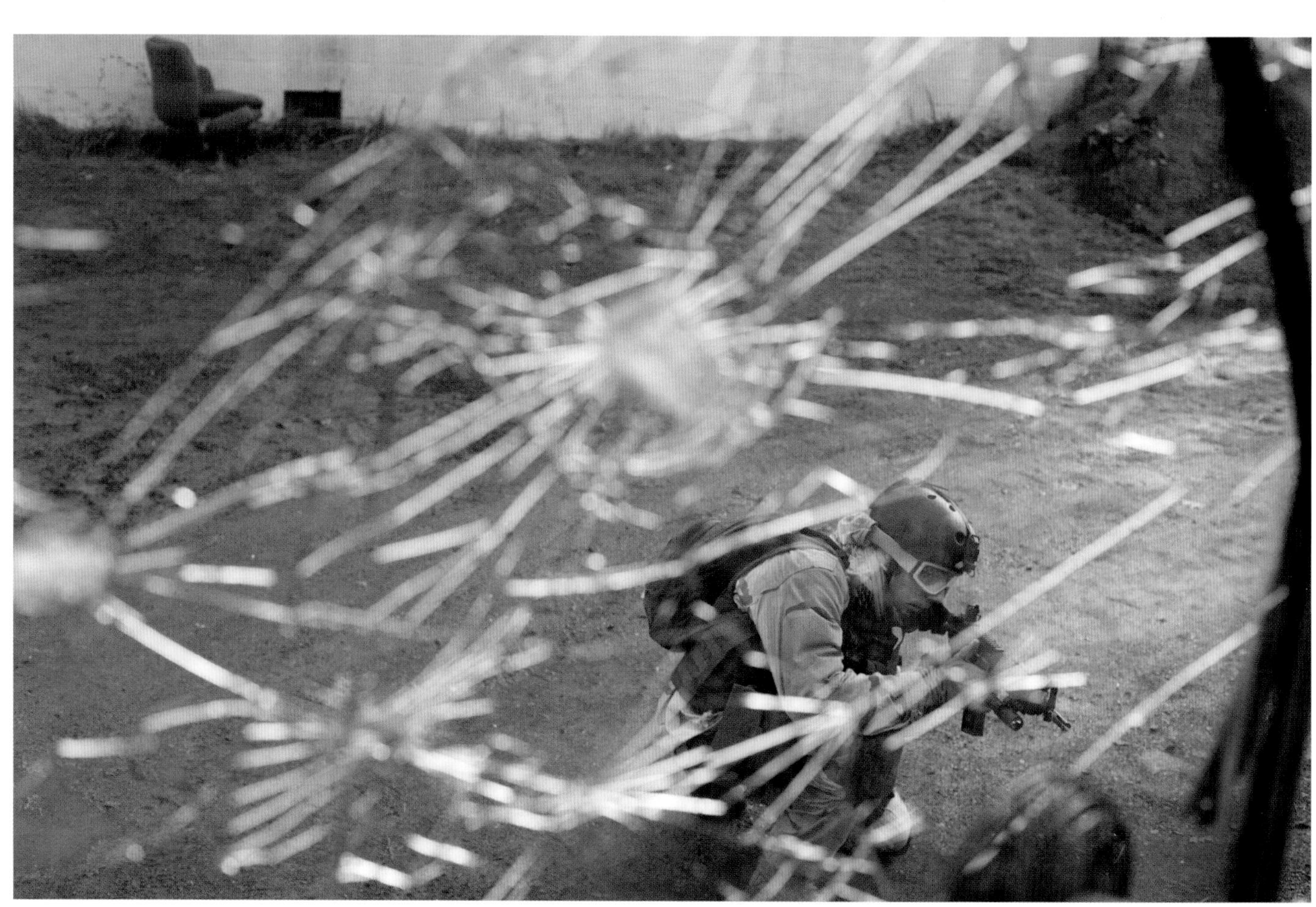

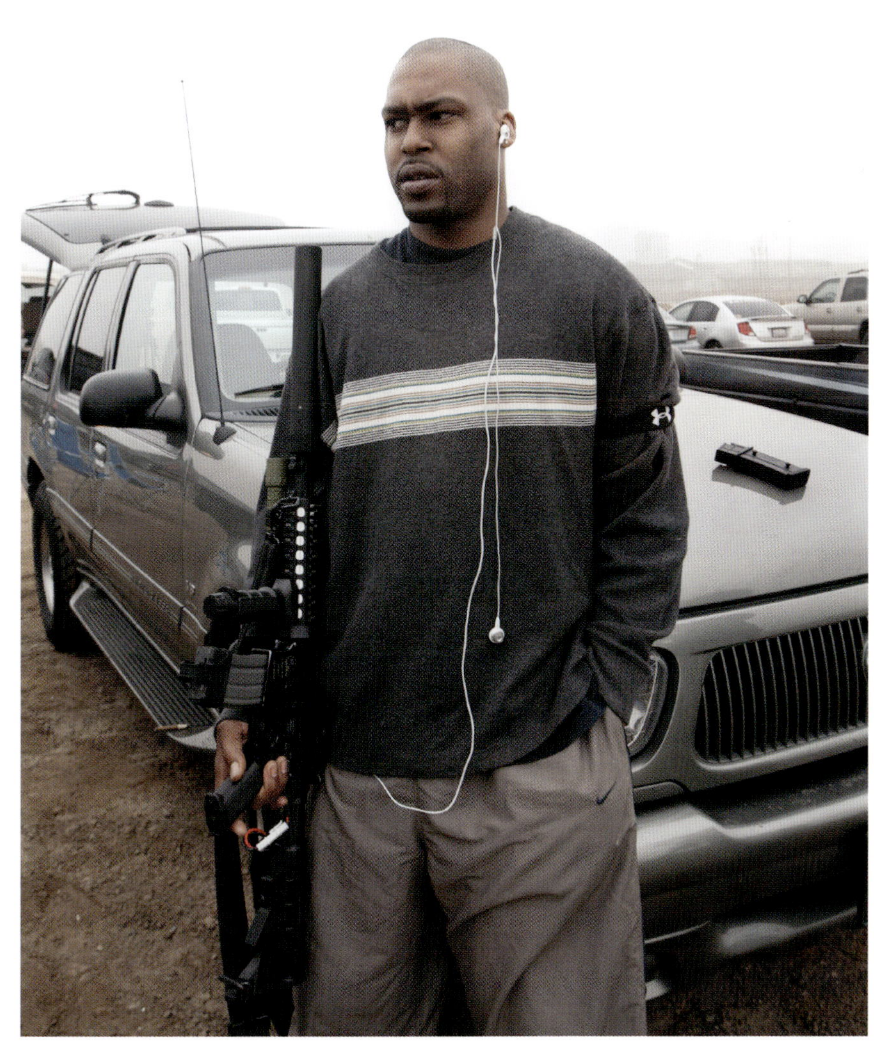

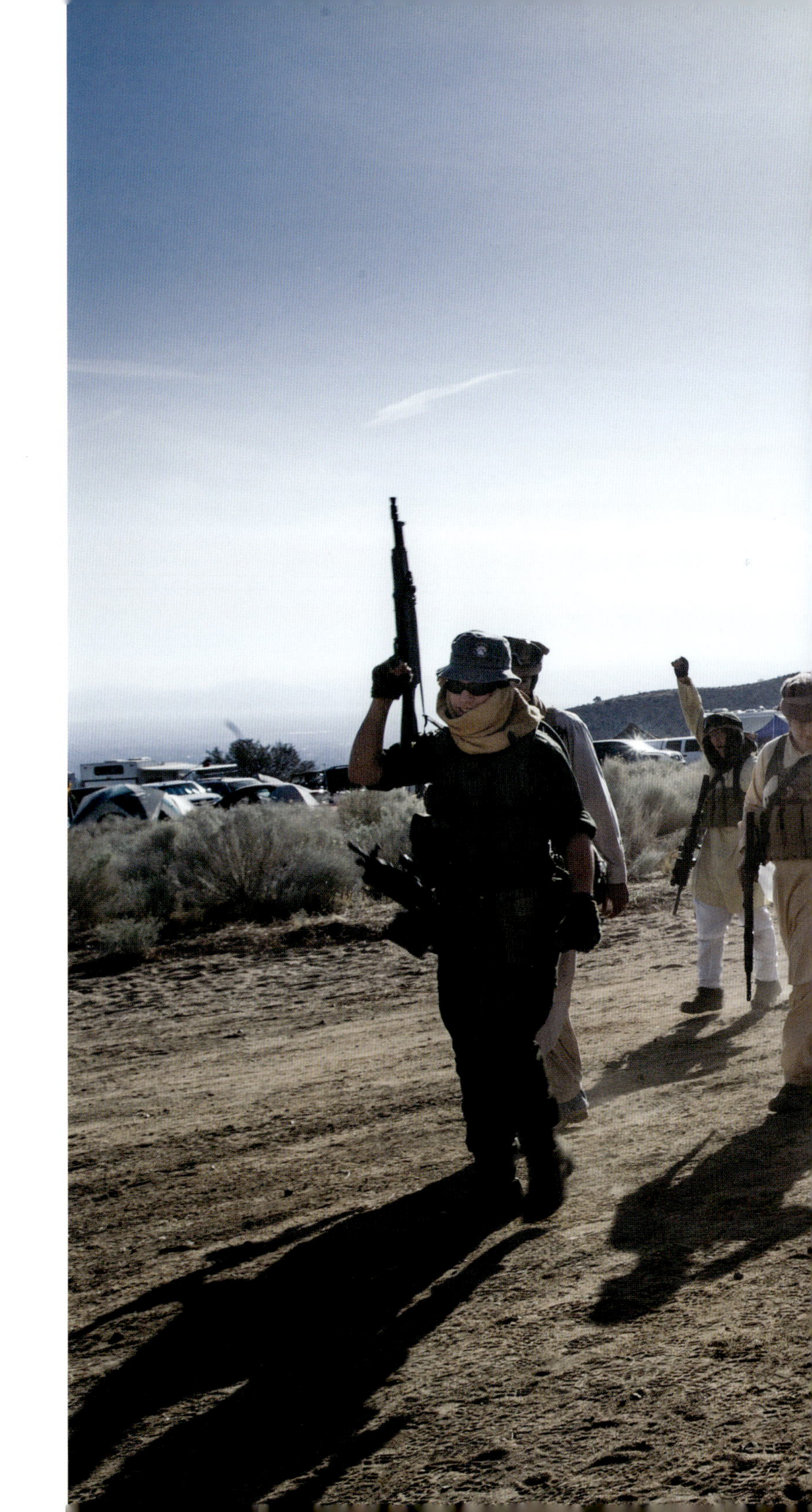

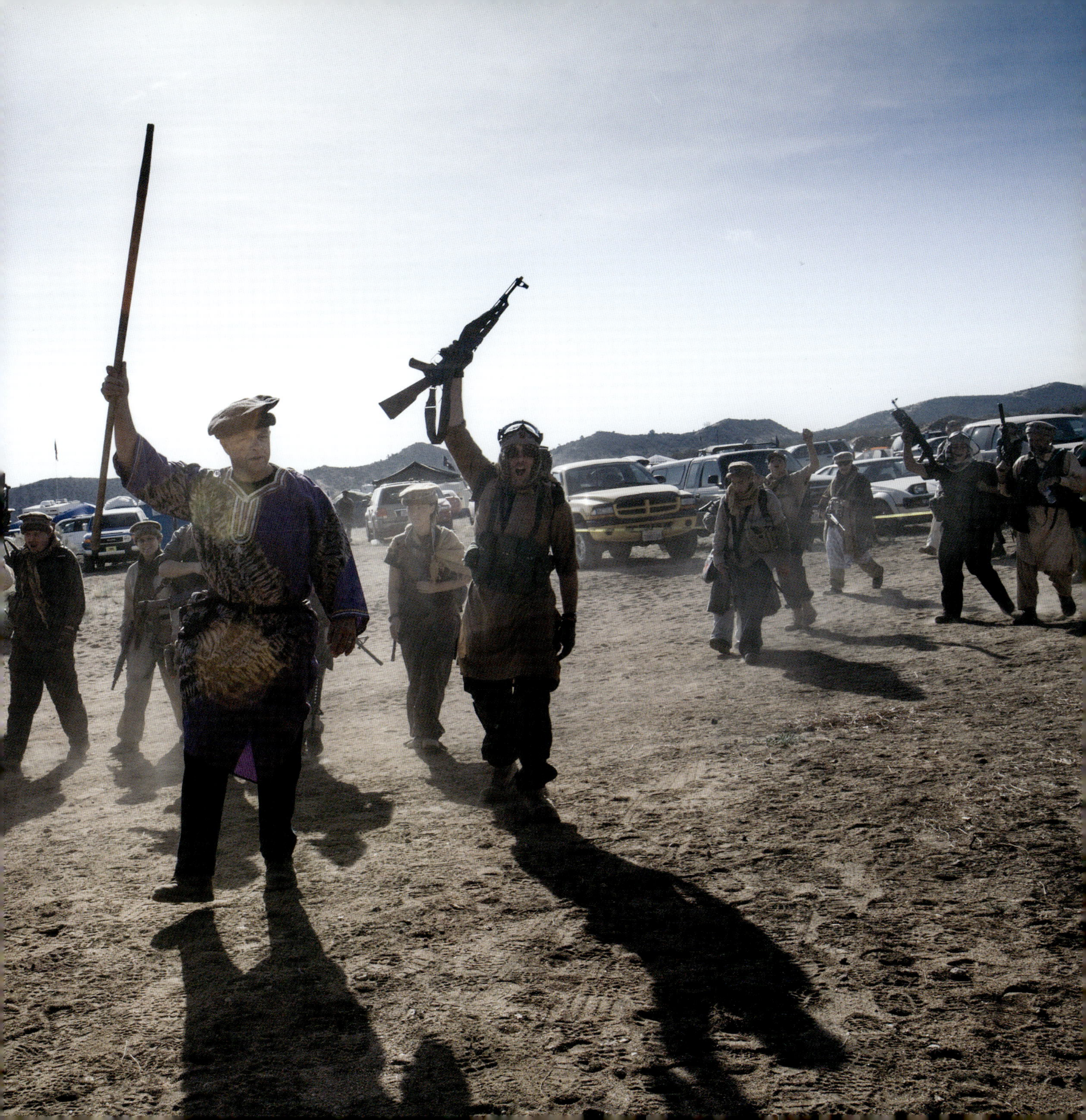

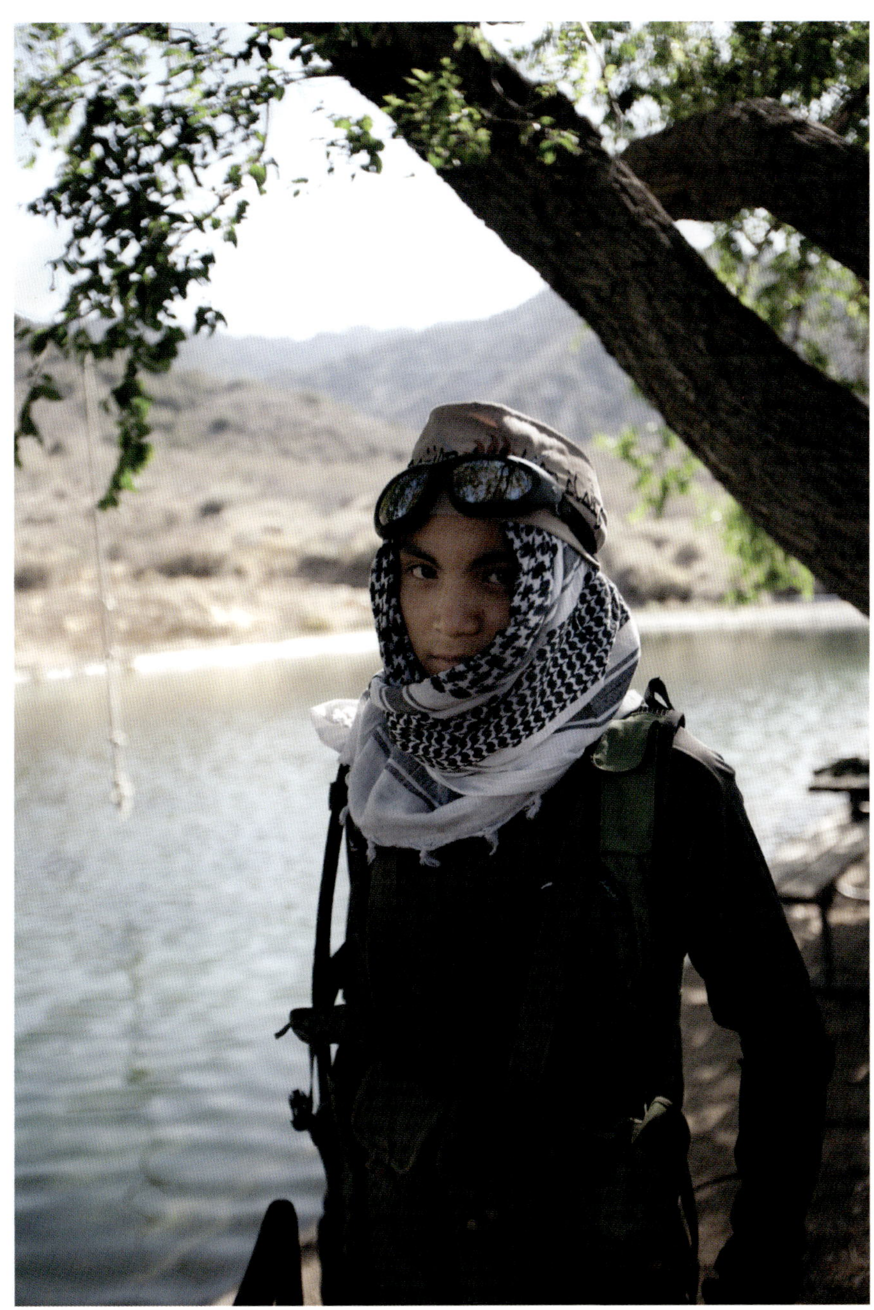

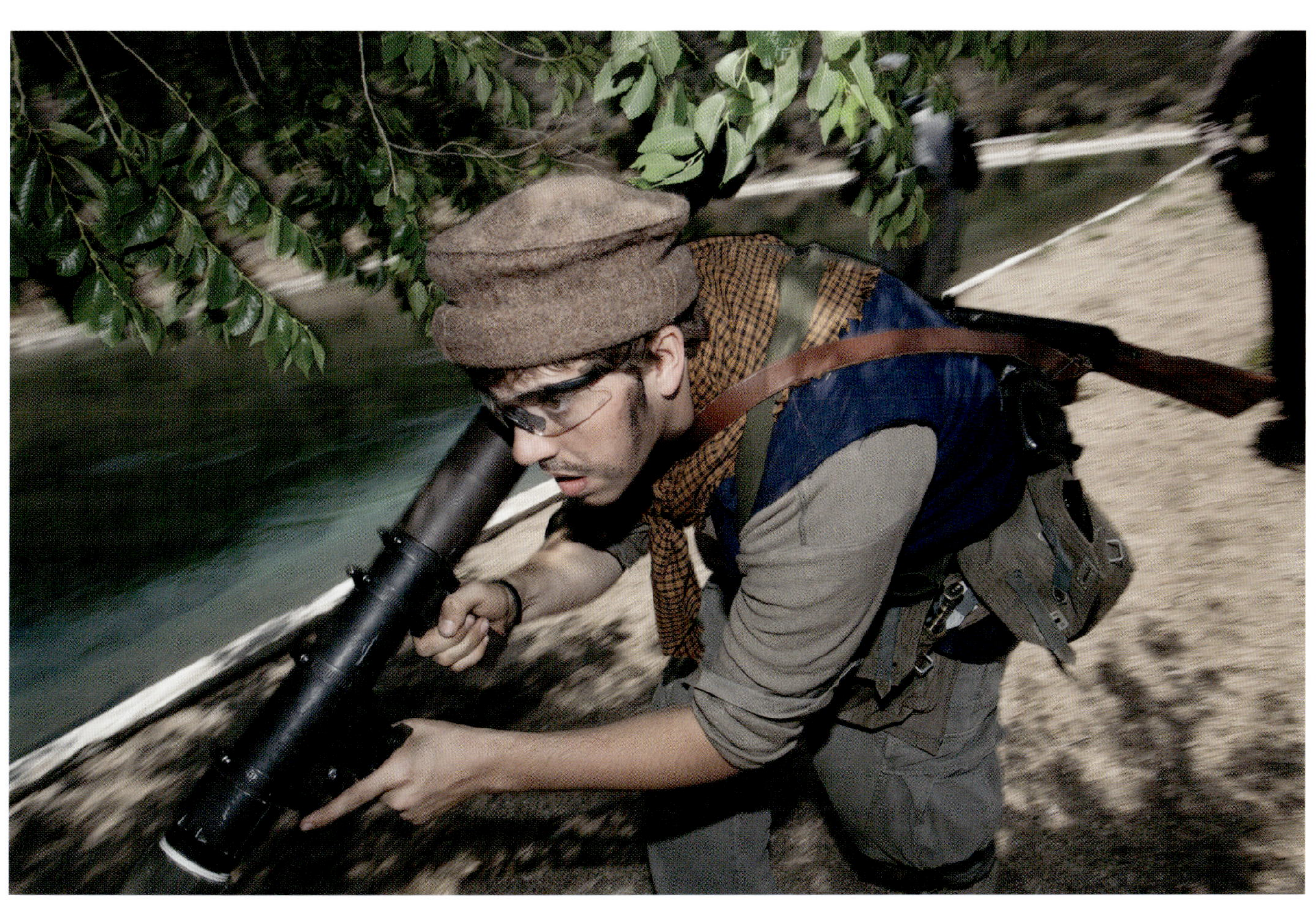

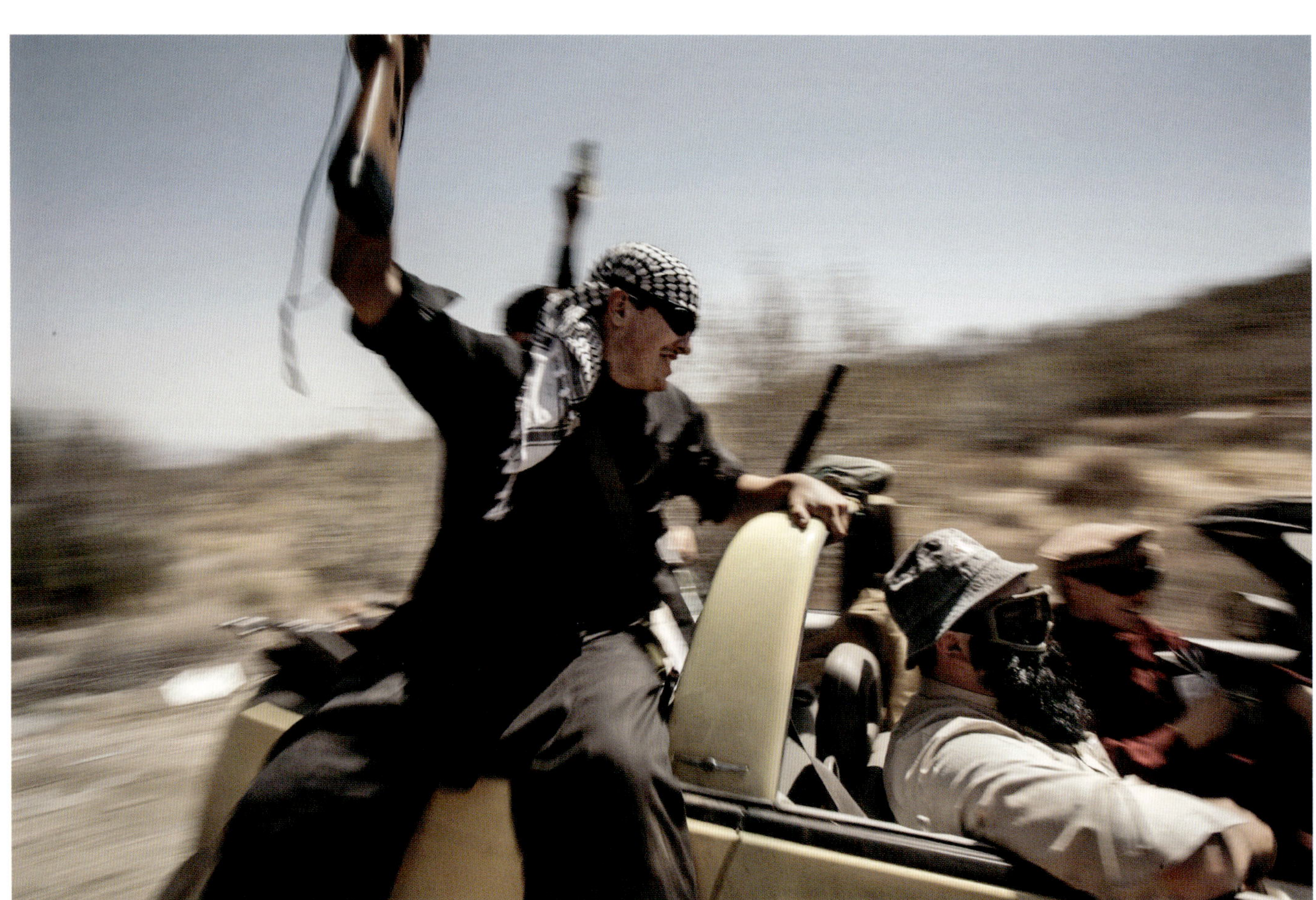

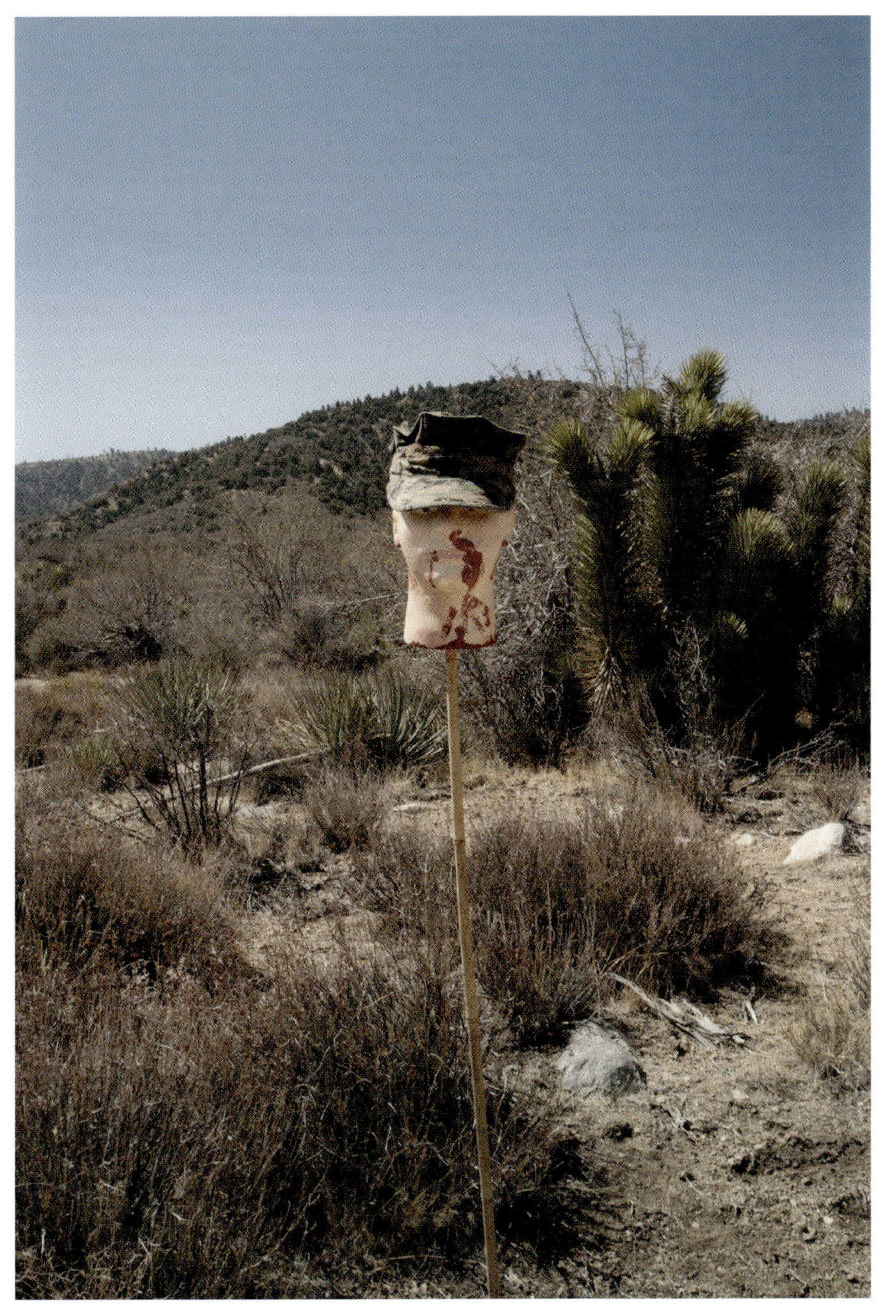

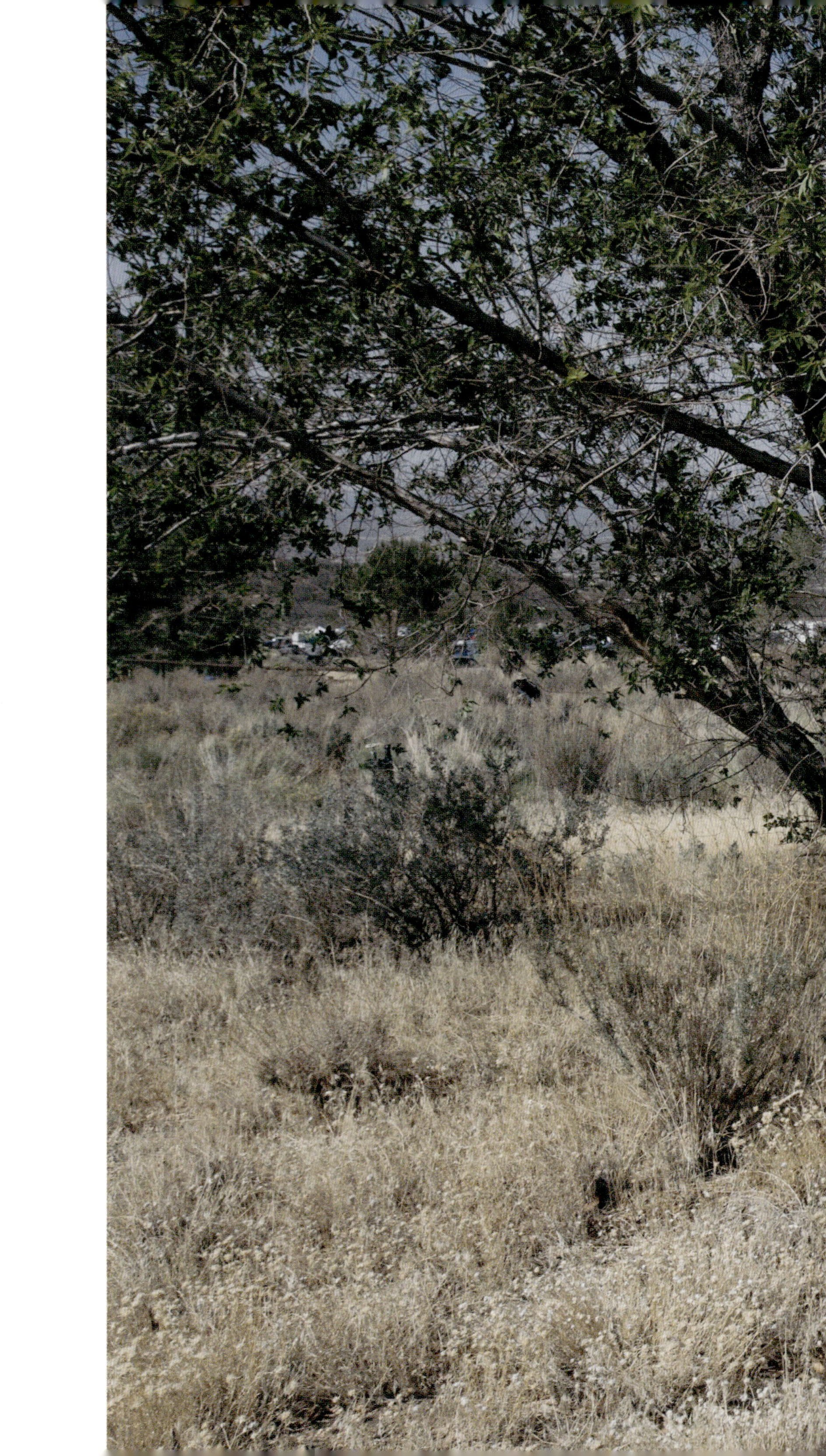

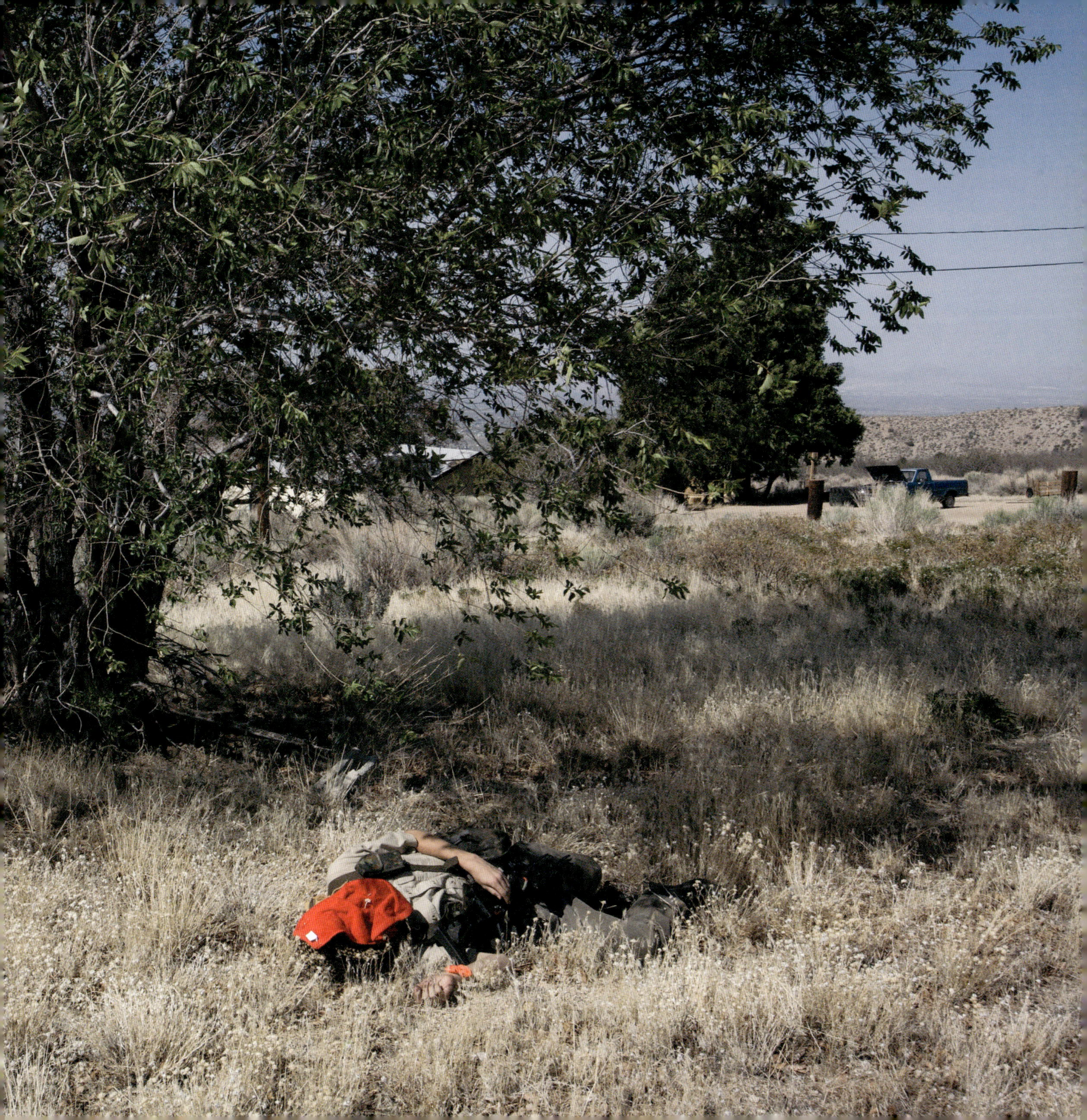

POINT OF VIEW
Meredith Davenport

This work began with a paintball game I played with two journalists who were on a holiday break from the war in Iraq. At the time, I wondered why two guys who were so immersed in the "real" violence in Bagdad would want to run around and get shot at with paint.

I have followed violence and destruction all over the world. Many years ago I spoke to a nun in Uraba, Colombia about the lasting effects of the rampant violence there on the children in that region. She said that children learned early on not to trust people they did not know and not to smile. They had to hide any emotions because sometimes the smallest gesture could betray those close to them to their enemies. The nun worried about the long-term consequences. The conflict was creating a generation of kids conditioned by its contorted values. At the time I made the photographs in this book, the United States was deeply engaged in wars in Iraq and in Afghanistan. While these wars are very different from the one in Colombia and very far from home, I wonder how the contorted values of conflict are brought home to us. You cannot live in the United States and not know someone who has been involved in warfare in one way or another. The web of links from these wars to my own life astonishes me. My ex-brother-in-law served in Iraq. He returned home, traumatized by his service there, and killed himself. My dear friend Quil, who I was playing paintball with, has lived in war zones for the past 10 years covering Iraq and Afghanistan for the BBC and NPR. He has seen many friends and colleagues hurt and killed, some of whom I knew as well. A childhood acquaintance died early in the war when his Air Force fighter plane was shot down. Thousands of men and women are returning from war zones wounded—inside and outside. How do we as a society absorb the rage and violence carried back from these distant conflicts? Is it possible to metabolize the effects of violence and war through popular culture? Are these games a way to understand conflict more intimately or are they desensitizing us and helping to perpetuate a cycle of destruction?

After the paintball game I began to research contemporary war re-enactors and came across the Airsoft community. Airsoft is a game of invented scenarios played with replica firearms. The guns shoot small plastic pellets. Games are inspired from a wide variety of themes but they often have a military training component. I traveled all over the country to photograph games where players dressed in pajamas and homemade costumes chased each other through the barren winter hills of Northern Virginia or the tropical forests of Florida, in "The Hunt for Osama bin Laden" or to document the fictitious death of Fidel Castro. In a game I photographed in the desert outside of Los Angeles, California, hundreds of men fought behind retired military commanders to defeat unnamed Arabic-speaking tribes. I also recorded interviews with the players and organizers of the games. The photographs, interviews and videos I made became part of an archive of materials that I have worked with in different ways on exhibitions and performances for the past five years-all with the intention to answer and explore these early questions I had during that first paintball game.

Some of the men I met playing Airsoft games were veterans from Iraq and Afghanistan, struggling to fit back into a society that admires the idea of soldiering but is scared of the reality. One veteran said to me, "People close to you really don't want to hear about how many people you have killed." Some of these veterans seemed to be searching to re-create a sense of fraternity from their military experience—even if some of the binding agents for that brotherhood—like terror and loss—cannot be re-created in a leisure game. There were young men testing out the idea of being a soldier and older men who knew they would never be "military material," as one player put it. They wanted to feel what it was like to be a soldier without getting killed. One player believed that carrying around a replica of a big gun gave people a sense of power and confidence in other areas of their lives.
The player's impulses and curiosity to experience violence and fear are not far from some of my own impulses as a photojournalist. The camera is a way for me to feel empowered and in control of the world around me. It is also an excuse to experience the intensity of uncommon emotions. I think that is why I have always resisted making a judgment about the morality of these games.

I became fascinated with the way players and event organizers imagined and translated the threats so far away that were depicted in the media. In one game, the head of a mannequin had been removed, painted with splotches of red and placed on a stick with a camouflaged hat that is clearly part of the American army uniform. The horrible beheadings in Iraq that were being shared on the Internet were now part of the players' imagination of this conflict and of the game. Many of the locations and narratives in the games were pulled from media headlines and news imagery. An abandoned wine cellar in Fresno, California became the location for the game "Kill House" and one of the most poignant images in the series. In the photograph, a young boy stands handcuffed in a square of PVC plumbing pipes. His head hangs low and his shoulders are slumped. The boy's submissive gesture and the gruesome walls of the wine cellar echo the mood and texture of the photographs of captives being tortured in the Abu Ghraib prison in Iraq. It is as if a part of him has absorbed and internalized the images referenced.

I made many of these types of news images. I remember speaking to a colleague before leaving a job in Central America with a wire service. I told him I was leaving because I needed a change. He replied, "Why are you leaving? You are just going to make the same pictures wherever you go." I think he was talking about an unspoken aesthetic formula that has been created over the years. These formulaic photographs are like a visual thesaurus of suffering. There are certain images that are expected from particular news events. They are part of a narrative of war and trauma that has been unconsciously agreed upon by the producers and consumers of news. They echo previous iconic photographs. In war photography there are many of these images—dead and wounded bodies being cradled before death, close-ups of dirty, war-weary soldiers with leathery faces, and inconsolable families slumped over the lifeless victim at a funeral after a military attack. Every natural disaster tells the same story visually with epic wide-angle scenes of destruction punctuated with tighter shots of human agony and heroic rescue efforts. Every political protest must have a photograph of a screaming face in the foreground and flags and banners in the background accompanied by a photograph from above of the masses of protesters. As I was making the photographs in *Theater of War*, I was aware of how I was re-enacting these images through my viewfinder just as much as the players in the game were re-enacting the images they had seen in the press.

During this work I became more sensitive to the web of news images, symbols, and icons that are part of a subconscious system of visual language we use to share our experiences. Like a popular television show that becomes a constant topic of dinner conversation, these images are both familiar and distant. We are so far removed from their original intentions that there is a latent frustration. A desire, in a world saturated with images, to experience the world more deeply, for something that feels true. •

INTERVIEW WITH PARTICIPANT 1, INSTRUCTOR
Meredith Davenport

MD: What do you do here at the shop?

P1: Well, I just do the event planning with J, and I don't really work at the shop here although I do spend time here, but I just help him plan events.

MD: How did you get started in working with Airsoft?

P1: Well, when I first got out of the army about three months back, I worked at a place called Northwest Tactical. It was this big warehouse with about eight buildings inside the larger warehouse, like a miniature city, and it was going to be this training area for SWAT teams and police response units, and National Guard and reserve units. The government agencies pay you on their schedule, which is like the end of the year, which doesn't really make you a lot of money fast enough so we started doing a lot of Airsoft stuff, and that's where we started making the money. That's how I started running events, and that's how I got into it. Once the place folded I still wanted to run events because it's fun, so I started doing it with J.

MD: Talk a little bit about your experience before you were in Airsoft, about your experience in the military?

P1: Okay, well, I joined the army at eighteen in 2000. I signed up in 2000, and I went to basic training in January of 2001. There's a kind of military tradition in my family. I mean my grandfather was in World War II, my father in Vietnam. It was just that was what you did as a man at that time, and that certainly was not what they pursued later on in life. Yeah, so I went to the army at 18 years old. I went with an infantry Ranger contract. I went to my basic infantry training OSUT, One Station Unit Training, which is like 14 weeks, finished that up, sat around and waited, got my first test of waiting in the army for about three weeks and went to Airborne School, which was surprisingly easier than I thought generally.

MD: Did you like it?

P1: No. I mean okay, you know what, I like hitting the ground, and then going like "oh, man, oh, I'm a man!". You know like, I have this gun, and I jumped like death from the night sky dude. You got to do it now. I like that part. And I enjoy being in the plane where everyone is screaming and these red lights are on and you get amped up. It's very exciting. But the moment you actually step in, all you really do is you get in the line of sixteen guys and you just walk out the door. Everybody just walks, and then makes a turn left, and steps out the door, and that's it. So if you stick yourself in the middle then there is a lemming effect and your brain doesn't really think about it until you've hit the door, and it's too late. And at that time it's like: oh no, bad idea, oh, too late.

MD: So how long were you a Ranger?

P1: I actually well, yeah I'm still… there's another story to that. But my third day of the Ranger Indoctrination Program was a little different than other special operations forces I know. The deal with the Ranger battalions is that there are only three of them. It's kind of small I guess; it's like the lowest rung on the special operations ladder. It's the guys who shoot stuff and carry heavy things—other guys do more intense stuff. The training actually takes a long time because you go to something called RIP, which stands for Ranger Indoctrination Program, which was three weeks, and it's now four. All that they really do is take about 500 people, and whittle them down to, maybe, 100 by doing things like saying they will do a lot of physical tests, you know stuff like that, and they weed people out that way. They will also give you a lot of time off, and they will say things like, "Don't go to X bar in Columbus." Sure enough, fifteen people would go to X bar, and all the instructors will be there, and it's fifteen people off the list because what they realize is that whoever it is that you hire for this job has to operate in the real world, and you can't give somebody this enormous ego trip who is not even an adult yet. You get this enormous ego trip and then I mean, you know, the minute some kid graduates RIP, he is in the bar going, "I'm an Army Ranger, I'm going to kick everybody's ass." So you do that, you go to the battalion for about six months to a year, and then they send you to the actual Ranger School, and when you come back you're really part of the club. You're, of course, part of the club even before, but it's a different level.

So you do the whole process, maybe take a year and a half to two years before you're completely in. They're not going to kick you out for something small any more. You're part of the team, and now you're in charge of something, be it in and out of it, two- or three-men team, four-men fire team, things like that. So that was the whole process with that, and I did that for four years, and I got out in January 2005.

MD: Well, talk a little about the training you're giving the guys today?

P1: Okay. Well, the stuff we're doing today was really just some pretty basic stuff that I have done before, not something we did a whole lot of because we really didn't—that's not the purpose of… that's not the specific mission that that unit was assigned to do, but it's something I'm familiar with. What I was really trying to focus on are not individual skills, because if you look at the pictures you know you've got guys standing up in the middle of the firefight. You've got people wandering around. We have people in a big cluster in the middle of an objective. What I really wanted people to learn was some basics of how a team operation works. I mean, really, we're using something that everybody likes but in any organization there are many phases of whatever it is that you're doing. I think by the end of the day they realized that okay, well, we've got to go where we're supposed to go, do what we had to, and make sure we did what we needed to do, and then leave. You know some people asked me before, like this is weird, do you feel like you're essentially teaching people how to be these stone-cold killers? And I really think that's ridiculous because honestly, it's just outrageous. You know people think it's really easy to walk around with a gun and shoot people, and believe me, all over the world there's people with absolutely no clue what the person who walks around with guns and shoots people is doing. But to do it right… right, I don't know if there's a right way, but you know, to do that job to a high level of proficiency is, I mean you could spend years. Me and my friends kind of joke that we have a master's degree in shooting stuff, and I mean you think about it and some people go to college for four years, kind of part time, and you get a bachelor's. I'm like, you did this for four years, every day, yeah.

MD: Talk a bit about that because you were telling me this morning about how difficult it was to make that transition from leaving the military.

P1: Well, it's really hard because I'm now this ROTC [Reserved Officers Training Corp] cadet. I took this army scholarship and I'll be going back in 2010, as one of the oldest lieutenants ever I'm sure, because they're normally 21. I will be really old, like 28. My brother said to me that the problem with you guys, with Rangers, is that you have this patch that everyone sees, that you wear around, that says, "I'm a certified bad ass." And everyone believes it. Like when I graduated Ranger School, my brother actually made for me and all my Ranger buddies T-shirts that said "100% certified bad ass," and we thought it was this really cool gift. But it does kind of ring true. And then all of that just, like, goes away because when you walk out anytime, you leave the Ranger compound and on Ft. Louis everybody sees you and they look, and they're like "that dude is …"— but you know those guys will be looking at you. They have been in the army 17 years, and you've more stuff on you, and you've done more stuff, and been doing what the army does, because essentially what the army does is kill stuff. I mean you can say whatever you want, but that's what the army does. They fight and win wars, and that means killing people. And to me, it's almost unfathomable to anybody who wants to join the army to not kill people. Like when people say I joined the army because I, like, really wanted to do something good, like I wanted a really good job. Why would you—you could do that at home, man! Go work for Warehouser or something, or get a job with Microsoft. I don't understand. I know there are important jobs that people need to have, and I have probably calmed down a bit since I have been out, but you've got this whole thing that's built up that says you are the top. It's like guys who are on the varsity football team in college, or in high school. High school is over, and you're not on the varsity team. In my case it's my choice. You know at some point you decide, no, I don't know if I want to do this anymore, and the thing is, all the reasons that I left for, it's all there in the real world. You just don't realize that because you never really grow up. Housing is paid for, food is paid for, healthcare is covered, so it's almost like being in mom and dad's house still. And you get out, and you realize the stupid bosses and silly rules and bureaucracy and job dissatisfaction is all there. So you might as well just do something you're really good at. It's kind of how I feel.

MD: Is there any kind of comparison between what you guys did today and what you did when you were a Ranger?

P1: I use a lot of the same techniques as far as teaching—like, walk, or crawl, walk, run type stuff goes. That's in the army. They use it a lot—because you know, you start people very slow with some really simple stuff. You kind of move them up to that walking phase, and and then into the running. The techniques are similar. The method of teaching is similar. There's so much other stuff included in how you have to execute that correctly that people already know, because they're a Ranger in the Army, and they already know how to hold the weapon correctly, how to do a mag change in a second and a half, how to cover a sector of fire, how to pick up their buddy's sector of fire and it's the myriad of things that have to be done, you know. They don't have to decide who is on special teams on the objective because they have already known, for like three months, who is doing what. And they have already customized their equipment so that they're carrying the things that they need to carry under the objective. I mean the difference is, I could just talk about what you have to do to actually take down the vehicle and get people out of it—that's it. There is a big difference, but for the most part the spirit of it is the same, it's just the details change.

MD: For instance, this morning when you were doing the takedown of the vehicle, is that something that I could have seen you doing in Ranger School?

P1: We actually won't do that in Ranger School because Ranger School oddly enough is not part of the Ranger regiment. It's part of the Army. They call it Ranger School actually, I think, to keep women out: that's really why I think they call it Ranger School. It's essentially a leadership school. They make it really simple on purpose because you're not eating, and you're not sleeping and now you're being graded on how well you lead a bunch of hungry, tired people so that makes sense. But in actual range of time that's something I have done. I mean in Afghanistan I have spent some time doing stuff with VCPs [Vehicle Control Points] or I think they change the name to, like TC, TP—traffic control. It's hard to keep up with all the acronyms.

MD: So describe step by step what you did, just so I can put that behind the pictures...if you could share some of that.

P1: Oh sure. As far as, like, what were you actually doing during takedown?

MD: What were you doing? What were you teaching them to do?

P1: Well, the first thing was that they realize they have a squad, which is anywhere between 8 and 12 people for the purposes of Airsoft. See this is where the details just change but the elements are really the same, and they're going to have one element that's pulling security from the front, and then the other fire team is going to approach in buddy teams with a buddy team per door for opening of the vehicle at such an angle that if that security team does have to fire, they're not firing into them, and that they're somewhere they can get away quickly. Then you just approach the doors in buddy teams, and bring the passengers out one side of the vehicle. In actual operations we have done it kind of whichever way it works best. But what you pick up, like that doctrine, is very rigid and that's not always the way it happens, but it's a simple tactic, and we're using people who don't have a lot of experience, military experience, or any sort of experience of that nature. You've got to do it the simple way and it's easy, and it makes sense and is easiest for them. In the real world we can tell when we've secured the vehicle and when no one is doing anything, and we know that if somebody moves the wrong way we can drop it, in point seven seconds or something. Sometimes they will be bringing people out of both doors, and whatever doors, and sometimes you can use common sense and figure out what's going on. I mean we pulled over families on picnics and, well, a guy's not really going to take his kids to go to car bomb or something. I mean there's times when common sense applies and times when it doesn't. It's hard to compare that to the real world but for the most part that's pretty much the deal. Pretty much all of these tactics involved one element providing security for the other one while they maneuver; opening the doors, pulling passengers out one at a time out of one side of the vehicle—securing them, silencing them, speeding them to the rear. And so a lot of that stuff is lifted directly. I guess what we call TTP, Tactics Techniques and Procedures, is lifted directly, just the detail is changed. There's things that don't apply, you know, like, with the guns, for example, with Airsoft guns, I still don't understand all the things that can go wrong. I'm not so great with the electronics, and you know there's a hundred things that can go wrong, and there's no way to know what it could be. With a real gun there's the jam that could be easily fixed or your barrel explodes, so it's either you're done or you can fix it, and that's it. You know with Airsoft guns there's no way to know it. So there's just a lot of stuff that changes, you know. The Rangers obviously have penetration power. I mean BBs don't go through cars. BBs, they don't really go through trees. That's about it. It's pretty much, the moving parts are there.

MD: Why do you think people play Airsoft?

P1: Well I think people do it because it's fun. I guess why do people bet on a fantasy football— because that's what appeals to them. Why do kids go play cops and robbers. I think it's obviously a mostly male hobby. There are not a lot of women that are engaging at all. My wife comes and plays sometimes, but she's an exception to that rule probably. You know because guys like guns. They do. Men are raised to like guns. I was raised in a household with military guns and look what happened. I just had this anthropology class, and they did this whole thing about gender roles. We called them gender roles because that's what they are. Men like guns for the most part. Guys have this fascination with guns and cars and sports. Maybe not all of them—I'm not into cars, but I'm into sports and guns. It's hard to explain, I mean there is my wife, you know, why does she like jewelry? I don't get it. I really don't. You know, I'd rather have something that works. I just don't understand, but I know she likes it, and that's really cool to her, and I bet she couldn't even tell me why it's cool. I mean it's probably just been engrained, you know, after years and years and years, that girls like jewelry and that's what they like, and that's what we're getting them for Christmas. Maybe it's like, I like guns and that's impossible to say. I mean people play it for so many reasons. There's the military people that I met that play it. I don't really play it. I can say I do play, but I don't, mostly I run the events. Mostly I like to run things, put things together, help people out, guide things along, and share any knowledge I have that might be valuable. I just hang out with people who appreciate a certain segment of my life that some of my other friends may not appreciate. For me that's probably what it is—that there are people who kind of appreciate a certain part of my personality that other people just don't get and think it's rude table conversation.

MD: What do you mean?

P1: Well, I mean it's taken me a long time—if you had met me two years ago, I would have been a much angrier, less polite, probably more foul mouth kind of a guy. I've really been working on it today actually. I haven't said the F-word or anything, like, maybe more than twice.

MD: Is that because I was there?

P1: Oh, well, yeah. First big day, I mean there are a lot of reporters there. J runs this business. I don't want to make his business look bad, of course. I'm trying to do it less because I hear that it makes you look stupid, and the last thing I want to do is look stupid.

MD: What do you think in terms of the way that these guys appreciate this aspect of your personality?

P1: My parents definitely complain about it a whole lot. It's like there were stories that I think are appropriate to tell about my previous life—which is mostly like four years in the army now and probably two and a half maybe three years at war—that are not appropriate to other people. Like that really freaks other people out, and it doesn't bother me. I'm actually at the point where gore movies bother me again, and I'm kind of like before. It's weird sometimes though because I will watch gore movies, and I will be like, "Yeah, but that's fake. What you being all squeamish about dude?" It's hard to really explain, but I kind of worked myself back, like I can be, kind of, how I was before if I want to, although it's mostly just fake. I mean if the situation calls for me to be more polite, I can be more polite and be offended when I need to be offended and stuff like that. Not that I consciously think that I'm doing it, but I think my brain just realizes where I'm at, and who is around me, and how I should be acting. Yeah it is just things I would bring up that would—I just didn't realize how down they would bring people, or how shocking some of that stuff was to people. I mean I didn't know for a long time. I think for me—you know for a while there, I think I thought the same things obviously about killing, anything involving that sort of stuff, was funny, that it was really this big joke and I was showing everybody how apparently level headed I was by joking about it. But I don't think that shows people how level headed you are. I think it makes you seem kind of weird. My wife pointed it out to me and I think I argued with her at first. I mean to her credit I probably thought she was wrong, and now I'm saying she is right so hopefully she doesn't see this.

MD: Do you think these guys understand a little bit more or they just don't mind it?

P1: Most of the guys, at least on the team, on J's team and my team—I hang out with a lot of teams, but mostly with J's team—they put on the best events out here, as far as I can see, and I've been to a lot of events nationally. They're pretty good guys and we're actually pretty close. We hang out quite a bit, and yeah, I'm—I don't know if I have this—I was a gun team leader. I was in charge of three men, and on my last deployment to Iraq my really good friend, who is actually one of my Privates as well ... one of my subordinates was killed in an ambush and died while I was giving aid to him. So this is something I don't, like, I don't share that with a whole lot of people, but I do share it with some people when I think it's important. They understand that there is a real cost to war, and these guys get that. I think sometimes there's people who maybe have heard that story from somebody else about me and think that that's cool, and it makes me really "hard" because somebody I know died. And I don't think that my friend's death is a punch line to my life or some sort of neat backstory. It's his life, and he died, and his family has to deal with that. And it's hard to explain. It's definitely affected my life in a huge way. I guess I'm pretty strange and atypical on my politics and I honesty don't like to talk about them a lot because I don't really feel that's my role at all. And I could have sat with friends of mine who will say whatever their disparaging views may be of our government or President or whatever and, my personal views aside—which are pretty strong—I think everybody should have the right to free speech and say what they want. But if you're a solider in the United States military, you shouldn't say that—you know there's this guy, the lieutenant on Port Louis—Ehren Watada, or whatever—who said he wasn't going to go to Iraq. Did you hear about that?

MD: No, but I heard about the situation.

P1: Yeah, and a lot of people ask me about that and I guess they thought because they know me I would be fairly liberal, that I would kind of agree with them, and I just thought that it was was kind of ridiculous… if I signed up, and it really drove me nuts—I mean that guy was on ROTC and he graduated on ROTC, like 2003 or 2004. At some point while he was on ROTC he knew there was a war on, and he chose to go through with it because, believe me, there's plenty of ways you can get of our ROTC. I mean you could pretty much just say, "I don't want to do it. I'm gay." You wouldn't even have to say that, you just say, "I don't want to do it; enough." And they would probably let you out of it. And what just blew my mind is that he chose, I feel like he must have chosen to go through with that to make the statement.

MD: You think he was trying to get out of it.

P1: No. I think he was trying to make a statement—

MD: Oh, he was. Oh, I see, okay.

P1: Have you seen, *The Life of David Gale* where the guy, Kevin Spacey, or some anti-death penalty activist, frames himself for murder?

MD: He was just grandstanding?

P1: Well, maybe not, maybe he had a bunch of different reasons. But I feel like—he wasn't a private in the U.S. Army. He was a Lieutenant. There's 40 people who are supposed to—he is supposed to be everything to them, and he just said, "Screw you guys." I think it's illegal.

And it just—it's so hard. I think that's why—I don't think it's as severe a case, but I mean that's why all of Hitler's generals were all reluctant to kill him, even when they realized what a horrible person he was, and I'm sure some of them are horrible people too, but let's face it, a lot of them were probably just soldiers. And they were like, "Oh, I don't know about killing him," you know, because that's the soldiers' job: to do stuff, to do that. That's part of the reason that I want to go and be an officer in the Army. Because I just look at the leadership and think do those guys spend a day, like, they didn't—they went to college for four years, and let me tell you ROTC is a blast. But, like, it blows my mind. The friends of mine that I have in ROTC are going to be officers in, three or four years, and they're going to be in charge of people, and they're going to go to war and people are going to die.

MD: Because—

P1: Because of the decisions they make, right or wrong. You know it took me a long time to realize that my friend didn't die because of me, a long time, because I made a decision to put him in a particular position that night and he died, but it really wasn't my fault. I mean, somebody would have died. It just so happened that I put him in that position and it was him, but it took me a long time to figure that out. I don't know if I fully grasped it yet, and it blows my mind. Like now, next time it's something I can be more ready for, you know.

MD: What are the good things about being a soldier?

P1: Well, the teamwork. I mean nothing really brings people together like the threat of imminent and horrible death, really, that brings people together. There are a lot of my very best friends, my best Ranger buddies, guys who were groomsmen at my wedding and stuff, like my buddy Lou, I'm godfather to his kid: we wouldn't even be friends. I grew up in Wisconsin. It's as wide a disparity as you can get. My buddy Lou is Hispanic from San Bernardino. We'd never hang out, but we were roommates, like, forever, and I went down, and hung out with his family on the weekend sometimes. We would drive down for 18 hours. His mom would make us beans and rice and stuff. We go cruising around Hollywood which is a big deal to me because I'm from Wisconsin, you know like Brett Favre is right there next to Jesus. Although I don't know what that's like because I'm a Jew, but I mean he's like the lord and savior for everyone from Wisconsin, and that's about as cool as it gets. So yeah I mean there's definitely that. I see people, our friendships, who wouldn't normally have friendships.

MD: Here as well, in Airsoft?

P1: Yeah, well, we've got Mike who is married like me. He is a roofer. He is about my age, 25–26 maybe, you know. And then we're all friends with like a 19-year-old kid in college and a couple of 17-year-old kids in high school, and then we've got another guy in the team. He's a 31-year-old technician, you know, so that's weird. You had these friendships with people that you wouldn't normally have friendships with, and you definitely do stuff. I like putting on the events together because it's actually more difficult, because the Airsoft game doesn't really adequately simulate what's really going on. I mean this one wasn't too bad today, but a lot of sucky stuff happens in between the exciting parts, a lot, and that's probably where you become closest. But I think putting the events on together—there is a lot of sucky stuff before the event happens, and especially our big ones, where we've got tanks going this way and trucks going this way, and 15 jeeps that run out of gas at the same time, and then they have to be somewhere in 15 minutes, and if we don't have all the players they will get on the jeeps, then they are not going to get to the bridge in time for the big show, with the explosion. This is a small version of what they have done at other events, where they're up with little sleep for three days. You know at your beck and call, doing every sort of weird scripted thing we want, like walking into ambushes, like 15 times, which is not fun. I mean obviously you just have to know you're going to get shot, and have to walk down this road like you don't know you're going to get shot, 15 times. I remember the school we did this summer; they got blown up then ambushed, then blown up then ambushed, then blown up then ambushed, you know like 15–16 times all day. Because we just had these groups that we're cycling through, who we're training on these tasks, and they would just go to teach little sections and train on the task, and these poor guys were wasted. There's definitely a lot of that camaraderie, which I'm sure there is in any hobby.

MD: It seems stronger. I mean this is one of the parts that I really find interesting about it. You know it seems a bit stronger here.

P1: Well, I think it attracts—I mean I'm sure that's attractive to a certain type of person. I know there's a lot of people who want to see what it would be like, that they want a little taste, but they don't want the whole sandwich. It's like war is an appetizer or something, like we're hors d'oeuvre, I don't know. So there's definitely those people who have that kind of mentality. You don't see a lot of lone wolf-type people.

MD: We were talking earlier about how it seems that the people who are drawn to Airsoft versus paintball… maybe it's a little smarter, a little bit…

P1: I couldn't comment on paintball. I know there are distinct areas of paintball that people are interested in. I know there's two areas of paintball: there's sport ball, where they wear the BMX jerseys and stuff, and then there are the people who like to play in the woods. I guess they call it Woodsball. The military simulation stuff. My image of those people is that they are mostly the kind of people who play paintball, like maybe, twice a year.

You know you take all the kids out, and they all go play paintball twice a year. It's fun but that's it, whereas Airsoft is by far, like, I don't think there's really a lot of places where people just go and play Airsoft on a whim. It's definitely one of those hobbies, probably like historical reenacting. I did some of that when I was in high school, and it is definitely like that. It's one of those things you don't just pick up and put down. People invest money and stuff and they buy a lot of gear. I don't, but they do.

MD: Do you think that the popularity of Airsoft has anything to do with the fact that our country is in conflict, that there is a bigger presence of military images?

P1: I'm going to actually disagree with you, just because of what I know. Airsoft is huge in Asia and Japan and China. I mean in Japan it is enormous. They have these Airsoft teams that have dress uniforms and it's this huge deal. In the United States it's probably biggest in California, and in some of the eastern sea-board states with the most restrictive gun laws. That's plain and simple. Washington has very lax gun laws. You know we can pretty much go shooting on public land as long as you're being safe. I mean, who knows if people are or not, but we had pretty relaxed gun laws actually. You know a carry license is like 60 bucks or something. I mean it's as simple as going down to the Sheriff's department and applying, so I think that maybe a part of it—that's got to have something to do with it.

MD: Interesting.

P1: Because if you look at it geographically, that's the common thread. California has very restrictive gun laws, and it's this enormous forum in California so I think that has got something to do with it. It's really big in England. In England that's much bigger than it is here. You know, no guns in England. Apparently they're trying to restrict Airsoft guns in England. I don't think that's what people want. I think I would have to disagree because honestly I think if anything Airsoft may have become less lucrative because of the war, because people would say, I don't want to know if that's really, you know. I used to, maybe, feel conflicted about it, but I don't anymore because to me now it's so different, like the two are so far apart.

I mean, to someone else on the surface it may look like "Wow, that's pretty close to war" but that's a little scary. Trust me, it's not war because everyone has their moment in war, at least people who are in actual combat—you actually really, really realize it's not like in a movie and the main character is going to die sense that, like, you may not be Captain Kirk, you may be the dude in the red shirt who dies before the title, like the credits, the opening credits happen, like for real. Like you could seriously die and that's it, and it's over, and you won't even care about it because you will be dead, so there's that. And usually after you see your first person get shot or blown up or something, and you go: ooh, ahh, it looks like it really hurts. But it's so—then another thing, it is so weird to me. You can watch Saddam get hung on the Internet. There are videos that troops have taken in combat or people being shot on the Internet. How do you know I—there's been some news footage from various, I guess I mean, I really didn't want to—I don't want to sound all cheesy because I know I told you earlier if people say that they can't tell you what they did, and I was a Ranger and I can't tell you what they did for the shit, but I would like to be honest, I would say that I've definitely seen there has been footage on the news where friends of mine have seen themselves on the footage. I don't think anybody else would have known they were, but there were a couple of key things that happened in the war where they showed some footage. There were kind of media circus events—

MD: Fallujah?

P1: It doesn't really matter. There were some things that were—I'm thinking of one particular event, that was really turned into a media circus, and somebody was kind of made out to be something that maybe they were or were not, and there's all this footage from this dramatic mission involving this person, and there's friends of mine going, "Oh dude that's me" you know, and that's so weird to me, watching that on TV. You know it's weird to me to be there, and go to a communication center and hop on my email and call my wife, that's weird. In fact I would avoid calling her when I was there, and I know that sounds really horrible, but it's really hard to do the job the right way when all you're thinking about is what's at home.

Because for me I wouldn't say it's bliss, but you just reach an in the zone moment that you reach as a solider—and it's not where you make yourself brutal or it's not like *Apocalypse Now* or Martin Sheen, it's like watching a snail crawl along the edge of the razor. Well, I mean, that's a great movie, and it's fun to freak people out with that scene, but it's like—you get to a point where you're not as concerned whether you live or die, what you're really concerned about is your Ranger buddies, and how you as a team acquit yourselves on the field. That's what you start to care about. You stop thinking about yourself, and I think you're actually better at your job, and possibly you're safer to be around, when you stop thinking about yourself and started thinking about the team. And when you reach that, it's scary to realize when you come home. A scary thing is to realize when you reach that point and it's like, "Wow, how many doors was I the first guy through that didn't have anybody behind them but could have?" You know, how many IEDs were there that I drove by that didn't go off? How many bullets? You don't think about it until much, much later, but that's a good – I guess we can reach that point. It's a good point to be at I think, it's really hard. The difference between the two things is so enormous.

MD: What would be some other misperceptions in terms of the way the media portrays soldiering, or even how they portray Airsoft?

P1: Okay, well, I will do Airsoft first because it's easier and quick. I think Airsoft actually doesn't get too bad a rap in the media. I think what does get a bad rap is your softwares and parents who buy their kids Airsoft guns, and they're not paying attention to what the kids are doing, and then the kids get shot and everybody goes, "Ooh, its Airsoft guns." And I'm like, "No, that's bad parenting." You know what, my 6-year-old kid is not going to have an Airsoft gun. It's that simple, you know. If I don't want my daughters to dress like Britney Spears, we don't have a TV. My parents didn't have a TV. It worked out good for me. We talked a lot, but you know what I mean. So I think that's my whole deal with Airsoft in the media—I think the media coverage I have seen up here it has been pretty fair. Sometimes people sensationalize stuff, but they sensationalize everything.

MD: I mean more about, like, how, like, maybe—

P1: Or perceptions of people?

MD: Maybe yeah. The perceptions that people have of being a soldier and maybe

mistakes that they make about what they think.

P1: Yeah, I would say that people have a myriad of perceptions about Airsoft, so they're probably all right to varying degrees. As far as being a solider, well, there's a lot of different ways to be a soldier and I guess there is a difference between the soldier and the warrior… in fact the word 'soldier', if I'm not mistaken, there's an alternative definition to the word soldier, which could be a verb, which means to suffer, to trudge through it, and suffer on. And I think I looked it up once, for some paper I wrote for some class that I figured I can get an easy A by going "Ohh, I'm like this disgruntled vet, but give me an A." I guess it's kind of a cheap shot – but I think maybe the misperception is all soldiers are the same. They all do the same thing. What they do, anybody could do it. Does that make sense? I think there's definitely a perception that the people in the military today are the people who couldn't do something somewhere else, and I won't say that there aren't those people, but I bet you could look around at any job and find me someone who can't get a job somewhere else. I think there is a pretty even distribution of people—I mean I have met a myriad of people just within… actually Ranger regiments are a pretty white group, and it's probably about 60% white men from the suburbs, and then I think the second largest ethnic group after that would be Hispanics. There was just so enormous an amount of the different reasons people were there, the different reasons people did what they did, why did they did it, what drove them, what made them tick, you know. I mean, actually, all the ethnicity and background stuff, I think it's all on the surface. That's a good way to describe somebody because god knows what makes people tick. There's actually no way to figure that out.

MD: What's the difference between a warrior and a soldier?

P1: I mean, the soldier suffers on and gets through it, says, "Gee, I hope that I get home but I'm just going to do my thing," and there's nothing wrong with that, and I think that the soldier is a great title. I think the word 'warrior' is a little overused. I mean my word for it, that I use on my head, is a Ranger, because that's, to me, a very important word, and it's something that I always wanted to be called. I think the difference – it's hard to explain it, because it's not anything I have ever really thought of outside of my own head, but the soldier just kind of suffers through the stuff, and they do stuff, and they went to war, and that's really cool, and that's what they do. And that's good, and now they're going to go on with whatever else they did or they may say they are, but their job is—they have some job that's not taking other human beings lives, which in essence is what the army, what any military, really does. You know like there's this great quote in Von Clausevitz *On War*, which people with stars and bars and things on their shoulders really love. This is great, you know, it's like Sun Tzu's *Art of War* or something, and one of the first lines in the book is "war is an extension of politics through other means," and I think, I completely disagree with the whole book because—and you probably know because you covered at least some kind of war—actually you've probably been to more places where people were shooting at… you've definitely had a diverse spectrum of people shooting at each other, more so than I have, and it's just war, it is what it is. It's violence and conflict, as part of not only human nature, but nature itself. And I don't know why it happens. Why do volcanoes erupt? It's a very violent thing. It's disruptive to the environment. It's destructive. Why does it happen? I don't know. It just does. I wish it didn't happen, but then maybe—god, there is this book out there I've been meaning to read: *War is a Force that gives our Lives Meaning.*

MD: Chris Hedges.

P1: And I haven't read it yet, but I just really want to, because I love the title, and it does. I mean this conflict, it doesn't necessarily have to be war, but the conflict gives our lives meaning.

MD: Do you think that relates at all to anything that these guys are doing?

P1: Yeah, sure, the conflict gives their fun meaning, you know what I mean: their entertainment dollars. You have meaning because there's a conflict. I enjoy all kinds of movies, but there's got to be some conflict. I don't want to watch a movie about nothing. I want to watch a movie where there's conflict, and to whatever degree, whether it's emotional or whether it's external. I mean what's the point if not? Unless you're reading non-fiction and even then, even if documentary is not fiction, there's a story being told. It means people assume because it's non-fictional there isn't a story being told, and come on. Of course there's a story being told. I love it because there's this conflict. There's this balance of power. To see how people deal with that, and overcome it, I think it may tell them something about themselves they may not have considered.

MD: So do you think that some of what these guys do in the weekends could be considered sort of a way to get to know yourself better?

P1: Sure. I definitely think so. My wife does, she does mixed martial-arts with the little gloves and cage-fighting stuff. She's really into that. She really enjoys it. She is really good at it. You know I think she does it because she learns about her self. I mean she kind of said when I go in the ring, and you don't worry about getting in the cage and being someone else beating the crap out of each other, we might actually learn something, and I actually find that in life. Like I got married when I was 21, my wife was 19—I mean we are 25 and 22 now, or 24 and 21 now—and yeah, there has been plenty of conflict, and we probably learn more about each other after that fight or after that conflict than we would if we all just sat around and got along all the time, so sure, I'm definitely sure people do it to find out about themselves. I'm sure that I joined the army to find out about myself, without a doubt. I remember before I went, and in fact I think I probably thought it before I did the whole deal and became a Ranger, and went to work. When I signed up, I didn't know I was going to war. In fact I probably just thought that to be a Ranger sounds cool. Odds are Clinton is President, war, no chance, you know what I mean. Like nobody thought there was going to be war. My third day at Ranger indoctrination is September 11th and they told us planes hit the World Trade Centers, we're under attack. We're going to war. You guys are Rangers so you know what that means. And I was like, "No way, shut up. They're making this up man. They're just trying to make us quit." And I remember the next day they brought out newspapers and showed everybody and people just quit, like standing in formation, and people were just quitting. They're like "Okay, cool." I think I thought to myself this will be this cool experience where I'm going to find out about myself and probably what I didn't realize is you don't have experiences to find out about yourself, but what you actually do is you have experiences where you become something you didn't think you would be, that's what I think. The whole 'find out about yourself thing' is like… it makes it sound like you're going to write it down later or something. "Hey I found out the weirdest thing about myself the other day." That's not what really happens. What happens is you find out that you were someone you didn't think you were, that you weren't aware of. That, I mean, that's kind of my theory on it. I think there's definitely a lot of guys who, I mean god, there was some guy out there today, Eric, whose name I keep messing up. You know this is his first Airsoft event, and the guy actually did a great job as we put him in the squad leader position. He did a really good job. He is telling people what to do. He just kept them busy. He was managing effectively. I mean, I don't know what the guy does in the civilian life, but you know they generally find about themselves, and I think people may be more attracted to Airsoft because it's the closest you're going to get to next to military training equipment, which is not available. It's pretty close. It looks like it and it smells like it, and to the average person it might as well be. But to me, I realize there's, it's actually kind of bad for me because I started to develop bad habits.

MD: Oh really?

P1: Well yeah, because I think to myself, like, they're 200 yards away, they can't hit me, which doesn't really work in real life. I have to kind of cleanse that every now and then. It's kind of fake, and the re-enactors really like it, especially guys who would be into World War II and Vietnam re-enacting. They really like to go out in the woods and have these tactical stimulations, but they're just shooting blanks at each other. I did the "Brother's Day of War," and they would want to go to tacticals and I'm like, that's stupid: if we are doing a battle we should do it in front of people so they can learn. That should be the purpose. But these guys want to go out and test themselves in the crucible of combat, by firing expensive cap guns at each other, so I think for many people this is it, because the conflict is just provided by these little things that fly around in the air and hurt, you know. Whereas in other stuff it's just catharsis and I guess the conflicts are over other things, like the stitching on a regimental code for the continental line or something. I mean that's cool if that's what does it for you. I kind of like stuff flying around. Plus, they are not real bullets so you know, relax, it's only Airsoft, right.

MD: Is there anything else you can think of that you would like to say? Anything about Airsoft or anything that I haven't touched on that might make sense to talk about?

P1: No, I think that's it, and relax it's only Airsoft. You know what I mean, it's—that's all that it is. It's just— it's probably as bizarre as any other hobby and probably a lot better for you, at least health-wise. I mean that's about it. It certainly promotes a outdoor lifestyle, and I have seen a lot of people who started playing at a certain body size and they are at a very different body size now, you know, at a different level of physical fitness because one day they say, "Well, I don't feel like I'm really moving fast enough, maybe I should run a couple of days a week." Yeah but that's it. Relax, it's only Airsoft. •

INTERVIEW WITH PARTICIPANT 2, GAME DEVELOPER
Meredith Davenport

MD: I'm recording. Could you narrate what is going on?

P2: Currently the red side is trying to find glow sticks, orange glow sticks, to complete the mission. Each team has, I think, six glowsticks a piece and blue force has green and they both have to go through the town, find the glow sticks and return them to the re-spawn point to win. They are scattered throughout here, some are easy to find and some are rather difficult.

MD: How would you describe Airsoft?

P2: It's playing war like when we were kids, for grownups without all the real bullets. It's a psychological stress-reliever, being able to shoot someone else without hurting them. It's a sport with plenty of running, jumping. It's one of these things that encompasses so much that it's really hard to explain. Everybody enjoys it for different reasons; for me it's just what I did as a kid. I played war in the backyard and now I can do it for fun as a grown-up.

MD: Tell me a little bit about the scenario today, the Cuban sort of concept that you came up with.

P2: It was kind of easy with Castro being quite ill at times. We created a scenario in which Castro dies of a stroke and his brother, Raul, is put into power and the cabinet ministers decide that Raul isn't strong enough to govern and that the people should decide. Raul has control of the military while the ministers have control of the police and a better relationship with the people, so a civil war erupts and America decides to take the side of the pro-democracy rebels. And ah... I'm sorry.

MD: That's ok, that's ok. You're doing great.

P2: We tried to create a fairly realistic scenario that you might see on CNN or Fox News. Give people something that feels like it was torn out of the headlines and give them some scope of world politics. But most of it is that some players have to get objective A, other players have to get objective B and they shoot each other. Essentially that is what it boils down to. We try and put a little more window dressing on it, make it a little more intelligent, try and make people think. Because for everything we do they could essentially just look on any news website and find the threads that we put together for this.

MD: Right. What made you want to do something on Cuba? Was there anything in particular?

P2: Well, we try and revolve around potential conflicts around the world and Cuba came up... with a quite long embargo against the island. What would happen if Castro did die? Would democracy take hold or would it revert to or remain a communist state. Each event we try and do something a little bit different. Somewhere else in the world. We do events ranging from Iraq all the way back to Vietnam. It gives people a wide range of styles and also it gives people a chance to act differently for each event. For the Cubans today we had a large contingency of players from southeast Florida who are Hispanic, who really got into it, speaking Spanish and all that. It kind of gave them a sense of, "This is my side and I can play to really win," whereas most Airsoft events are mostly the USA versus some bad guy. We like to try to pattern our events so that each side is equally right to themselves. We don't try to play favorites with any side.

MD: What do you think draws people to it? What draws people to Airsoft?

P2: I think a lot of it is camaraderie, comradeship, where people can get together, just have fun, just be themselves. Airsoft is one of these rare sports or events where people of all social status or economic level can get together and have fun without thinking about who is who. We have people ranging from high-powered lawyers to people working at McDonald's. Everyone can get along. We have geeks, we have jocks, we have women you know, young men just deciding if they want to go into the military. We have veterans. It's such a cross-section of our society. You can have conservatives and liberals playing on the same team, having fun together without caring about the politics and I think that is kind of the fun of it. By centering it on real-world events we kind of make people realize some of the politics and it kind of gives them the sense that, that... I don't know.

MD: So you are trying to give people a sense of the real-world events as well?

P2: Yeah, because I think if you boil it down … some Airsoft groups use myths and made-up names and made-up countries and while that is fun to me it kind of takes the focus away from real-world events. If you kind of showcase some of the events someone might actually take the time and research it and learn about it. Think about it without condemning it. Such as doing a game in Iraq, where half the force is Iraqi insurgents and the other is Americans, it gives people a chance, maybe for a little bit, to walk in someone else's shoes. It gives them the chance to not necessarily see their point of view but to maybe, you know, take a little more time to understand their point of view.

MD: Do you think the popularity of this game has anything to do with the current state of affairs? Like the fact that we are at war as well?

P2: Well, yeah, I think Airsoft grows, especially the scenario games that we do, with current events just because our country has become … I don't want to say militarized but … more security conscious. So many people are buying guns for protection or whatever and this sort of fills a gap that some people might... I don't know.

MD: It's ok. You can say whatever you think. It doesn't have to be a right or wrong answer.

P2: I think Airsoft just grows because of the realism factor. I think people really kind of crave a sense of danger, excitement—and it's safe. Most of life to people isn't safe. This is a place that they sort of can control—they can control their environment. They are the ones that can go out and protect themselves. They are the ones that have the guns. They have their friends there fighting with them so it gives them a sense of security in a life that has no real true security nowadays.

MD: Interesting. That is a really good way to explain it. What do you think are the most positive aspects of it?

P2: The positive aspects?

MD: Yeah, the best things about Airsoft?

P2: I would say what it really does is it just kind of brings people together. It sounds corny but I have so many friends now from Airsoft that they range from not just locally but throughout the entire state, even the nation. If I go to an event somewhere else it's like I never left, you know, we just shake hands, we're buddies and it's a good feeling … It really promotes friendship and one of the key aspects of Airsoft is honor because the Airsoft BBs don't leave a mark on you so basically you have to, you know, say, "Yes, I'm out, I got hit". It's like when we were kids, "Bang, bang you're dead." You have to have some trust in the people you play with, and I have that trust in most people I play with, and it's rare when you can have trust in people, you know. It's harder in real life.

MD: Oh really, you think it's harder in real life to trust someone?

P2: Well, you know in real life I think everyone is trying to do their best for themselves and their loved ones and I think we concentrate too much on ourselves and don't worry about how it affects the next person. Here a lot of people get the ability to learn what affects the next person because if they don't cover for them or they don't support them then they get shot, and so it kind of teaches people and hopefully maybe that would carry over in real life, in the sense that at work they are part of a team as well, at home they are part of a team … their community and stuff.

MD: And what do you think are the negatives, if there are any negatives?
P2: Oh, there are negatives to everything and it's how you take it. Everything can have a negative. Airsoft, the use of realistic weapons, is a danger because to police they are real. They look real, they feel real—you can't tell the difference. That is a big negative and it's up to us as a part of society to police ourselves. To make sure we are carrying the guns properly, that we are not letting kids use them. Honestly, I think the most instances of negatives that come out of Airsoft are the instances where kids get a hold of the guns and take them to school. They are playing around, but to a police officer or a principal it's not play. These look real and they can scare people and that's why we try to play only with adults. We try to educate people. We try to tell kids, "This is not something for you, maybe play paintball." Because it's more abstract and a little more family oriented because it's not as reality-based

and if they want to get into something like that it's a good route to go to graduate into something like Airsoft. But Airsoft really takes a certain maturity level. I can't walk out of my house with one of these guns. I would never dream of it. I think that's where the negative comes from: it is the danger of how people would perceive a group of anyone running around with realistic looking weapons and stuff.

MD: Anything else that I haven't asked about that is important to talk about or think about with Airsoft?

P2: It's healthy. I've seen so many people come out here and it helps them lose weight. It helps them become better people in their normal lives. As I said I think it promotes teamwork, which I think in our world is sorely lacking. Since we don't have a sense of security in the real world then if you can kind of take it and get some security somewhere that kind of carries over into the rest of your life. You can feel a little more empowered to say hi to somebody or to go for that promotion at work, or just try to do better in your regular life.

MD: So you think it builds confidence?

P2: Yes.

MD: What about it builds confidence? Is it the teamwork?

P2: I mean a kind of a jocular answer would be, "You get to play with big guns." I mean anything like that would give you confidence but I think it's… not everyone is cut out for the military. I know I'm not. But it gives me a sort of a sense of a sort of pseudo-level of military service that I sort of get to train with my friends, people I like to work with, do teamwork, try to achieve a common goal and by doing that it sort of makes me think in my real life, "Why don't I do this in my job? Why don't I try and work with these people who in my actual life, my career, my family life, I could depend upon in that sense?" I think teamwork is probably the core of a lot because it makes you think about the other person next to you and it's safe. I mean, like I said, not everybody is cut out for the military. This gives people kind of like a small glimpse of what it is like to work as a team in something like the military. Also I think that one aspect that is overlooked is that I think it gives respect to our military. A lot of people use liberal as a dirty word and make it sound like we don't appreciate the military but I wouldn't do this if I didn't have the utmost respect for them. I wouldn't design the scenarios that I do if I didn't have the utmost respect for the men and women who serve. I think it gives those who are civilians a chance to look through a soldier's eyes you know. Maybe they would be quick to condemn our actions somewhere else in the world, but this gives them pause to think: this is bad, it's hard to deal with and they deal with it the best way that they can, because Saturday when I was playing this Airsoft game I encountered similar problems. So I think it builds respect for our military, for those that serve our country. I'm not sure. I wouldn't necessarily say it builds patriotism or anything like that but I do think it makes you respect someone else, someone who does this type of job on a daily basis.

MD: Several people have mentioned that they thought it was a tribute to the troops in a way.

P2: We did a scenario that was set in Vietnam. Vietnam was close to me because my father was in Vietnam and I never knew him and it sort of connects me to him. A lot of people came out. Their fathers had served, their uncles had served, so it was a war they grew up hearing about and it gave them a chance to, for a moment, to understand what their father went through. You know, World War II is called the good war and stuff. Vietnam was this ambiguous police action that you know, somehow, we were the evil empire. It really gives people a sense that it wasn't about that. It was about thousands of men and women serving there, having to deal with a situation that was insane, that a normal person might not be able to handle, and briefly showing them that. Showing them what it is like to go down a trail at night. Worrying about getting shot kind of gives them more of a respect, more of an understanding of why their uncle might be unable to talk about something and it really... one of the best things was that we had people coming with their fathers, with their uncles, with their brothers who served, and it was kind of interesting because I could see the look in their eyes: like now you sort of understand, like now maybe we can talk about it, you can understand where I was at that time.

MD: Did you hear any stories where that actually happened? Where people were able to have conversations that they weren't able to have before?

P2: I do know of a daughter that brought her father out here and they seemed to really enjoy it. I think it gave them a connection and in our society it doesn't always seem that fathers and daughters always have that good relationship. It's usually fathers and sons and stuff, and I think it was kind of inspiring to see them enjoying something together. The daughter taking the time to try and understand something that is so complex and we were able to give her the opportunity to maybe look at her father a little differently, maybe with a little more respect. And for her father to go, "You know my daughter is maybe someone I can talk to about this." Personally I don't know of anyone afterwards, if it changed their lives or anything but it was nice to see that connection while they were here playing.

MD: I think many people have members of their family there. Do you think there are a lot of people who have family in the military in your group?

P2: Yeah, I would say that a good 60 percent of the people who are here have members of the family in the military, are in the military … we actually had about 20 people who are actively serving soldiers play today, or national guardsman, which is actually another benefit of it: it trains them, it gives them even better training than they might have in the army. It gives them that one extra little oomph that they might need but I think everyone has some connection to the military. I don't think our society can escape that. My grandfather served during World War II, my father served during Vietnam. I had relatives who served during Korea. I have friends from work who are still deployed after years to Iraq or Afghanistan so it's all around us. That's why we play with war: we play with toy soldiers. It's just part of our society to a certain extent and this is just an outlet for that… for me, I think at heart as a kid I did love sneaking around my neighborhood with a toy gun going, "Bang bang." And now I get to do it for real or not for real, but as close as I want to do it.

MD: But you never wanted to be a soldier?

P2: It's not for me. I'm a dedicated civilian. I thought about it and … at least I try and recognize in life what I can and can't do, and while I have some regrets that's not one of them. I don't know if I would have been a good soldier or not. I'd like to think I would be but I don't like to make an assumption because it's such a dedicated task. But that doesn't lessen my support or desire to see our troops treated the best, trained the best and brought home safely every time, and that's one interesting thing about it—I can still have my views and still hang out with people who have served over in Iraq or wherever and it doesn't really make a difference. We each come together for our own reasons and it just kind of gets left at the door. I might be playing next to a die-hard conservative and next to him is me, a bed-wetting liberal, but together we are a team, we fight, we work together, you know maybe somehow we understand each other a bit more.

MD: Someone suggested today that this might be a good thing for people to learn to do in case, you know …

P2: I guess because I'm kind of pro gun-control I don't think that everybody should own a gun just because guns exist. I think like everything Airsoft should be regulated to protect minors and stuff, and I think guns should be respected enough that there is legislation to keep them out of the hands of people who shouldn't have them. I don't want to say that I believe in no one owning guns. I think that is a right we should have but I don't think our society is meant to have people who have guns that can shoot 800 rounds a minute. I don't think as a society it's safe to look at everyone trying to do something like this because then we become more and more paranoid. We become more and more empowered that, well, force could solve my problem. I think you can take security too far. I could sit for hours training how to defend myself, which takes away from the enjoyment that I could be having in life. To me if you give up, if you just center on security and nothing else, what is the point of living? You've just got to take that risk getting up every day. If it's gonna happen it's gonna happen. We can just try and make ourselves as safe as possible. I don't think Airsoft necessarily makes me any better at defending myself because Airsoft doesn't act like real guns. A leaf could actually block a BB so where I would take cover. In real life, it's not going to protect me, um, if I was getting shot at I would jump behind this wall, which is wooden. I'd be dead in the real world so it might actually hurt if you get a false sense of security, which is never good.

MD: Do you feel insecure in terms of the times that we live in?

P2: I just try to live my life the best I can and enjoy it because really you protect yourself 100 percent against something and then someone turns around and does something completely different. No one could expect or really predict 9/11 happening. No one could have really predicted Pearl Harbor. But then again some people could, but you could worry yourself to death worrying about every possible scenario. If you go too far with security what are you really gaining?

MD: Especially you, because you have a pretty good imagination. You seem to be able to predict a lot of things.

P2: It's scary because sometimes I'm watching the news and I'll be really getting into the head of a terrorist going, "Well, I would have just done this, this, and this… support would erode for the Americans and we would win." And then I go, "Wow am I actually really thinking that?" and it is kind of scary getting into making these scenarios because I have to have some empathy for the other side. I have to try and see where they are coming from and it's hard when some sides don't have that much good in them, but I don't think I could do this realistically or with any sort of honesty if I didn't. If I did an Iraqi game and portrayed Arabs in a stereotypical manner then I think it would be a huge mistake – not only an insult to Arabs but to the players, because it would reinforce a stereotype that would probably make them more insecure because they would miss any real threats. We don't get blindsided by stuff we already know, we get blindsided by stuff we didn't foresee happening. You know 9/11 happened because we actually thought that people would just take planes hostage and not use them as weapons of mass destruction, and how do you protect against that. You don't, you can't really because when you make a law against something, when you prohibit something, they are just going to look for something else and there is always something else. The next time it could be an oil freighter coming into dock with a nuclear weapon on board. •

THEATER OF WAR:
"A MASTERS DEGREE IN SHOOTING STUFF"

Esther MacCallum-Stewart

Soldiers are dreamers; when the guns begin
They think of firelit homes, clean beds, and wives.

(Siegfried Sassoon, "Dreamers")

Introduction: "Very bad form/to mention the war"

In 1933, authors, poets, and artists began to publish their work about the First World War to huge censure and disgust from the general public. What became known as the War Books Controversy allowed the public to see a series of now infamous poems, books, and art that helped shaped the landscape of literary war in the twentieth century. However, these texts were not received with the same adulation that they often garner today. Although we now celebrate the war poets for their hard-hitting portrayals of war, at the time, reminding combatants and civilians of the conflict that had just passed was seen as a shocking, disrespectful act. In the worlds of Osbert Sitwell, these texts arrived during a period in which it was "Very bad form/To mention the war."

Today, videogames are stuck in a similar position. While many feature familiar names or references to real events, videogame wars are usually removed from reality and try not to bring their players face-to-face with the ethical or political ramifications of conflict. When Atomic Games announced their intention to publish *Six Days in Fallujah* in 2009, a game based on the experiences of soldiers during Operation Phantom Fury, the response from the media and general public was so outraged that the game had to be cancelled. Unconsciously echoing Sitwell's words, Reg Keys, a father whose son was killed in the Second Battle of Fallujah said that the game was "very poor judgment and bad taste," going on to state that, "These horrific events should be confined to the annals of history, not trivialized and rendered for thrill-seekers to play out" (Keys in *The Daily Mail* 2009).

Reminding games players that there are real wars and real conflicts taking place during the course of their play is, therefore, still a difficult and problematic event. The *Theater of War* project deliberately challenges this interchange in a physical sphere, raising interesting questions about the relationship of the gamer to the text. The project is typical of the growing sophistication of gaming narratives, and the player's relationship to these stories. Wargaming, both in physical and virtual forms, has always been at the heart of many of the controversies surrounding videogames, in particular when negotiating the implied violence within the text and the subsequent role of causality upon the player. It is common, therefore, to see more complex arguments ignored in favor of the "violent games breed violent actions" strapline so favored by the mainstream media. *Theater of War* challenges this by implying that the player's awareness of this debate is a fundamental aspect of their play, bringing both real and virtual actions into direct contact with each other. Traditional modes of representing warfare as horrific collide with the deceptively adventurous approach that games often take. This essay examines some of the underlying principles inherent in Airsoft, LARP, and gaming communities, challenging the player/participant stereotype of vainglorious button pusher, and paying close attention to the ways that narratives of real and virtual warfare collide in difficult ways. It also investigates the link that two interviewees of *Theater of War* identify with directly—the connection between videogames and re-enactments of warfare.

In recent years, videogaming has not only become a dominant force in the entertainment industry, but has greatly developed in complexity. World spanning narratives and hard-hitting moral choices are becoming part of an AAA title's[1] remit, with players flocking to games that make them think or behave in thought-provoking ways. This "love" for games ranges from personal engagement with the dashing Ezio in *Assassin's Creed II* (Bioware 2009), to the passion and commitment shown by players of *Minecraft* (Mojang Specifications 2010–present). As a result, players are also gaining new forms of autonomy within gaming. These are most notably formed through their own behavior outside the text, which helps to shape the way it is perceived by others. Games scholars are therefore increasingly arguing that we should pay as much attention to how games are understood by the communities that surround them and the secondary output that they produce, for example through cosplay, fan sites, and fan videos (Newman 2009, Crawford 2011, Taylor 2012). As a group of people who are used to experimenting with the core text in a playful manner, videogame players are uniquely positioned to challenge the issues that surround them. For them, play and experimentation is inherent to the gaming experience, where the game text can be reformed, changed, or simply reset (Salen and Zimmerman 2004). The game is a liminal space where death means simply "restarting," and discovery is naturalized and playful. This attitude is crucial to the ways in which gaming is able to explore a number of important social, cultural, and political ideas. In short, gamers are used to manipulating the texts that they play with, and subverting them for their own ends.

The participants of *Theater of War* epitomize this. Their responses to the text are different, but impassioned. Rather like scholars such as Joseph De Lappe, Jacki Morie, and Mary Flanaghan, their objective is often to draw attention to the ways in which "real" warfare overlaps with "gamed" warfare, although their motives for doing so vary greatly. The photographs, players, and organizers interviewed bring self-awareness to their play, recognizing and understanding the implications of real-world warfare, while at the same time drawing attention to the unreality within the videogame. However, in the same way that the poems of World War I were (and sometimes still are) misunderstood, it is a fallacy to assume that the images in *Theater of War* simply decry or condemn games and warfare. Instead, they portray complex, heteroglossic responses to war that are tied up in issues of respect, empathy, and horror, as well as a need to understand the role that warfare adopts in modern society. More confusingly, they are also expressions of community and recognition of how warfare irrevocably changes beliefs. In a world where most people are not called to fight for their country, the need to understand warfare from the individual's point of view is often overlooked.

Understanding live-action role-playing

> *In a world, within our world, they'd created a world, unlike any other world...'*
> (Trailer for Knights of Badassdom, 2012)

LARP (live-action role-play) has only just started to be investigated by scholars, and critical work is often contentious because of the very different international approaches to it. One of the major reasons for this is the differing legislation for carrying weaponry around the world, which also affects "fake" or historicized weapons. In the United States, for example, groups such as SCA (the Society for Creative Re-enactment) take a "heavy" fantasy approach since throughout the society's history, different state laws have affected the use and type of weaponry available to them. While combat forms a large part of SCA events, players adopt long-standing persona, make elaborate costumes, and act out scenarios that range from calligraphy competitions to riddle solving. Participants are required to use "boffers" instead of weapons: large latex- and foam-covered rattan sticks that approximate real weapons in weight, but do little damage when they strike the body. Similarly, Airsoft guns are considered deadly weapons in several states and Federal Law across the United States requires that they are marked with an orange plastic tip on the barrel at very least. Several American states also require other criteria, such as pink or luminescent stripes to highlight their unreality. In the United Kingdom, this extends to guns used in computer arcades, which are usually made of brightly colored plastic in order to differentiate them from "real" versions; however, the use of historical weapons is less stridently policed, and ownership of the latex "hollow core" weaponry used in LARP events does not require a license.

In the Nordic countries, LARP is taken extremely seriously, and although there are many high-fantasy LARPS, others have little fantastic content and instead rely on the acting out of challenging situations, including extreme LARPs that discuss the impact of situations such as rape or apocalypse scenarios (Montola 2010). Stenros and Montola's excellent *Nordic LARP* describes these scenarios as "a loose group with numerous commonalities, even though there is no single universal denominator" (2011: 15). In the United Kingdom, LARP is largely a frivolous activity, although increasingly popular. High-fantasy, steampunk and "horror" LARPs are popular, with nearly 5000 people attending the Lorien Trust's annual *Gathering* (Lorien Trust 1991–present), and many smaller groups taking part in scenarios based on everything from the Victorian age to modern day zombie survival. Finally, many countries simply do not tolerate LARP or its derivatives. It is hard to imagine, for example, a LARP taking place in Israel or Palestine, where real-world situations occlude the acting out of more light-hearted (or indeed, more serious) scenarios. These different approaches mean that role-playing games are extremely difficult to discuss, and if LARP is difficult, its kissing cousin Airsoft is nigh impossible.

Neither re-enactments nor LARPs, Airsoft games fall somewhere between these and a sport. They are serious fun; educational and unreal; false and true. As with LARP and re-enactment, being a participant also carries significant social stigma, meaning that it is difficult to observe these communities or obtain interviews. Although all of these hobbies are becoming increasingly well-known, many participants do not wish to disclose their participation to outsiders. Interviews are further occluded by participants trying to justify or otherwise accidentally obfuscate their reasoning for taking part. See for example

Bowman (2010: 66–72) and Kowert and Oldmeadow (2011), research that suggests gamers actively maintain the stereotype of their subculture, but often do it through a Lacanian "Othering" (whereby they regard themselves as normative, but identify "Others" who they do not socialize with, yet are in a virtually identical situation, as strange) of different role-play or gaming groups.

Airsoft re-enactment or games (as opposed to Airsoft as a sport, which usually involves shooting at targets) is very physical, involving running, hiding, and chasing other participants. Airsofters use replica guns that shoot small, brightly colored plastic pellets. Many countries (and states) demand that weapons used are Airsoft accredited, rendering them relatively safe for use in such situations. The wearing of protective gear is mandatory, must cover the eyes, and often additionally protects the face and head, in the form of helmets or Airsoft goggles. Coincidentally, some of the more popular brands of Airsoft head protection are based on existing military designs, and also look very similar to the headgear worn in the videogame *Halo*, subtextually reinforcing the link between the two.

Airsoft takes place in artificial environments designed for both the suspension of disbelief and to make the experience varied and interesting. To comply with safety regulations and also to protect any participants or non-participants who might accidentally stray onto the field, Airsoft takes place at registered sites that may already have spent money on terraforming their land to provide bases, cover, scramble zones, and other obstacles. Airsofters must additionally be registered with a club or group to take part. As a result, Airsoft role-plays and re-enactments are not a public or spectator sport. Events are role-play "lite," in that although groups are often split into teams and fight each other, the narrative is limited to linear, military objectives—e.g., capture the flag, rescue the prisoners, secure points on the map. As participants discuss in the *Theater of War* project, the aim of Airsoft is often more serious—to teach people the nature of "real-life" situations and the skills involved, and to provide them with an idea of what it might be like to take part in combat. The events in which interviewees took part differ from many Airsoft sessions, in that they deliberately aim to re-create historical events or to replicate wartime situations and conundrums. Throughout, the emphasis is on re-creating techniques and the atmosphere of war, or playing through likely scenarios that might take place during combat.

The fast-paced, immediate nature of Airsoft means that it is difficult to role-play or even adopt a wartime persona, and most people do not do this, although on a basic level roles are often allocated according to experience, ability, preference, and leadership skills. Some events have tiers through which players progress, allowing them access to more sophisticated roles or activities, or rotate roles such as team leader, in order to experience a varied play style. Because of this, military Airsoft is the most common form, although some LARP groups also incorporate it into their events. In the United Kingdom, *E-Zero* (2008–present), *Distant Vista* (2004–present), and *Bigger Guns* (2005), all focus on post-apocalyptic or science fiction themes, and have Airsoft "sections" where the players don Airsoft equipment over their costumes and take part in more physical shoot-outs. These events are the exception rather than the rule, however. And overall, the issues of respect for both the weapons themselves as physical artifacts capable of causing harm, and ethical respect for the nature of soldiering (which is discussed below), largely preclude this adoption of fantasy persona.

Reading LARP—Magic scrolls and Kalashnikovs

The *Theater of War* project is interesting not only for its content, but also because it exposes a community for which very little research exists. Previously, LARP and re-enactment have always been regarded with suspicion by the general public as they quite literally involve the escapist acting out of fantasies. There is an intrinsic link with causality and effect by the media—in short, performing violent actions in an unreal scenario leads to violent emulation in the "real" world. One only needs to look at tragedies such as the Batman killings of 2012 or the Utøya and Oslo attacks by Anders Behring Breivik in Norway to see the press desperately trying to link serial gun crime to its fantasy counterparts, with videogames and real-life re-enactments in the front line. This has become so extreme that when Seung-Hui Cho went on a killing spree at Virginia Tech in America, notorious game critic Jack Thompson immediately blamed the game *Counter-Strike* before it was discovered that Cho did not have any games in his rooms and did not appear to play them. Airsoft, because it is a physical reality, is rarely even countenanced as an activity that "normal" people might wish to participate in. Sarah Bowman argues that role-playing in all its ludic forms represents a new development in cultural representation, self-expression, and provides a "healthy, useful outlet for creativity, self-expression, communal connection, and the development of important skills over time" (2010: 9). However, although an increasingly popular and diverse genre, the hobby is usually represented as consisting of social misfits with very few inter-personal skills, hiding behind the velvet sleeves of wizards (the skinny ones) and warriors (the more well-endowed ones), while women in need of sexual attention adopt the roles of munificent healers, rich ladies from Arthurian courts, or temptresses in chainmail so skimpy that it would be unlikely to deflect the measliest of blows. Articles such as "Parents forced daughter to have medieval duel as punishment" (McCabe 2011) and "At least they are getting out more" (Waugh 2012) epitomize the derogatory approach that the media takes to these activities. Airsofters are also regarded with suspicion; violent misfits with gun fetishes for whom each event is simply training for "the real thing."

The diversity of LARP means that research struggles to quantify such an internationally diverse hobby. So much so that the LARP described in the recent *Nordic LARP* anthology (Stenros and Montola 2011) bears very little resemblance to other LARPs around the world. Early writing on the subject tends to be journalistic rather than critical. In recent years, several attempts to investigate geek culture through rites of passage have featured the hobby—for example in *Fantasy Freaks and Gaming Geeks* (Gilsdorf 2009) and *The Elfish Gene* (Barrowcliff 2008)—both of which follow the authors' attempts to comprehend geek culture and reclaim their sense of self-identity. In recent years, however, academic interest for LARP as both a fan practice and a cultural text in its own right has grown. *The International Journal of Role-Playing* (Draken 2008–present), *Playground* (Hansen 2011–present), as well as events such as Solmukohta (Harviainen 2011, www.solmukohta. org) have helped to kick-start a growing critical movement, and writing in the area is now prolific. For example, JiiTuomas Harviainen's excellent summary at Solmukohta of 2011's publications gives a good idea of the diverse approaches that are now forming.

Warfare is a well-known topic in games. This is partly because of the links between violence and gaming already mentioned, coupled with attempts to support or debunk this argument. Critical studies of gaming narratives and communities are also popular, with an emphasis on clans and hard-core gamers, often thought to be first-person shooter (or FPS) players. In 2009, Huntemann and Payne's edited collection *Joystick Soldiers* examined the connection between the military and games in a series of essays, including writing from renowned war artist Joseph De Lappe, whose projects include *The Great Debates* (2004) and *Dead in Iraq* (2006). *From Sun Tzu to X-Box* (Halter 2006) investigates the continuing relationship of history and wargames, including an examination of US army recruitment tool and videogame *America's Army* (2002–present), whereas papers investigating everything from torture (Sample 2008) to realism (Payne 2012) are common elements of Game Studies. Numerous journals have presented special editions on the impact or ramifications of militarism in games, and it is rare that overviews of videogames or histories do not mention its influence at some point. It is not the intent of this review to discuss these in any detail, but instead to note that militarism and gaming are such common bedfellows that it is unusual to see them excluded from any full-bodied discussion of games, and to note that the majority of AAA titles still contain militaristic themes, actions, or overtones.

You had to be there—re-creating war

> *Bleed is experienced by a player when her thoughts and feelings are influenced by those of her character, or vice versa. With increasing bleed, the border between player and character becomes more and more transparent. […] Bleed is instrumental for horror role-playing: It is often harder to scare the player through the character than the other way around. […] A classic example of bleed is when a player's affection for another player carries over into the game or influences her character's perception of the other's character.*
>
> (the Viåker jeep designer collective, quoted in Montola 2010: 2)

The images created in the *Theater of War* photography project present a serious investigation of Airsoft practices. It is important that the project is seen as a performance piece, rather than a spontaneous moment at a live-action event; even if this is how the images depicted played out. If players are hyper-sensitive to their own roles within such events, they are also keenly aware of the implications this can have on outsiders. As I discuss below however, the in-game community often holds very different values to those of observers, and there is a keen awareness that issues of respect, patriotism, and representation may be misunderstood. Core examples of this include the differing attitudes to representing Nazism discussed by Thompson (2004); however, it is the seemingly more mundane discourses that take place during events which can often be more problematic. These can easily be misconstrued by observers. For example, many Nordic LARPs involve the enactment of difficult social situations and events, whereas UK LARPs set in historical periods may allude to racist or sexist sentiments. The participants are keenly aware that they do not hold such xenophobic ideals, but may feel that they are forced to express them. This can also be seen in the terminology used in the military, where xenophobic phrases or flippancy toward extreme events are commonplace. Participant 1 discusses how in the first year after active duty, he used to joke about his experiences and "death and killing" without really realizing how they disturbed others who had not experienced them directly. As he reintegrated into the civilian community again, he came to the realization that this made him "kinda weird." In these settings, such expressions are normalized through a sense of Goffman's frame analysis (1974), whereby the internally framed community recognizes the terms and situations as codified and therefore normative. So, for example, referring to death through humor is naturalized (although still not always accepted) and therefore becomes a normal part of discourse. Similarly, the representation or re-creation of situations that may seem extremist to an onlooker is understood within the context of the event, rather than as genuinely representing a visual embodiment of "true" belief. Once again, representation is not seen by players to inform causality or genuine belief—in fact quite the opposite is true and often events are deliberately created to provoke thought and challenge preconceptions.

These verbalizations sit uneasily with a players' own sense of "bleed," whereby real-life beliefs and role-played actions intersect (Waern 2010, Montola 2010). For most players, their consciousness of vocalizing such ideas or taking extreme actions causes discomfort; however, it is important to recognize that participants also have a keen sense of where bleed can help, or hinder their own personal development. In the *Theater of War* interviews, this is very clear, with participants describing their experiences in the abstract, and clearly understanding their roles as players. The thoughtfulness that results from this is produced by their efforts to avoid bleed but also to understand how experiencing such events can benefit them. A good example of both of these occurrences comes from Participant 6's interview, through his discussions about the merit of Airsoft events, which he does by describing the value for someone else (his son) and his subsequent analysis of the event, in which he expresses surprise that he ultimately chose a side he would not have expected. Debriefing or discussion after each event, in either a formal or constructed context, often helps players come to terms with each event, and helps them with the transition from artificial situation to real world.

Lastly, it is crucial to acknowledge that the transience of these moments means that they are often more meaningful retrospectively. At the time, a wry chuckle or an acknowledgement that the re-creation has taken place may occur, but it is only later that recounting the incident cements it within the imagination. As Jessica Catherine Lieberman argues elsewhere, the image is not a "real" re-creation of events (2008); more, the images and events of *Theater of War* give a more fulsome interpretation to Hynes' "imaginative retelling of events that are believed to be true." However, it is the memorialization of the event through image, anecdote, or recollection that becomes crucial.

Playing LARP—Being Private Ryan
It is important to situate LARP, REN (re-enactment), and Airsoft within a subculture,

which is increasingly becoming more socially accepted, that of geek culture. This group is becoming increasingly prominent, largely because of changes in media technology that have allowed the fan-producer to gain more autonomy. As early adopters of transmedial technology (Jenkins 1992), "geek" culture has established a foothold on the Internet that has allowed it to proliferate. LARP, REN, and Airsoft, as well as playing videogames, all fall into this broad subculture. Geek culture is experimental; with the mind-set that as a minority group already laughed at for their insular, nerdy obsessions, what do geeks have to lose by dressing up as clerics or playing *Magic the Gathering*? This means that many cross interchangeably between different aspects and are more open to performing apparently extrovert or unusual hobbies.

For example, many LARP and Airsoft players begin as tabletop players or videogamers, and want to extend their games in a more physical manner. This is true of *Theater of War* Participant 6, who talks with pride of the fact that he and his son are "running about outside" and spending as much time building the Worth Airsoft site as they do playing it. The progression of "static" videogame to LARP or Airsoft formation seems a natural progression here, and one which is described as physically rewarding in a way that videogames are not. It is also symptomatic of the growing popularity of kinesthetic videogames such as those on the X-Box Kinect or Wii. Physical interaction with videogames is not only becoming popular, but indicates their growing hybridity; the top selling games on the Wii are those associated with dance or exercise such as *Zumba Fitness* and *Wii Sports*. These titles are not even particularly game-like to play, belonging more to the keep-fit genre of instructional videos, albeit with a more interactive bent. If videogames are becoming increasingly physical and have a growing demographic, it is perhaps a natural progression that some players will want to externalize the non-kinetic games by acting them out somehow. This is especially true of those that involve complex activities in game, which nevertheless are achievable in real life. We may not be able to re-create Batman's energetic vertical climbs up the walls of Gotham's buildings, or the super-speedy martial arts prowess of the Monk in *Diablo III*, but we can use existing hobbies such as paintball, Airsoft, and LARP to re-create other gaming scenarios. As Participant 6 says, "To watch a 16-year-old stay outside all day, and work hard, and play hard before he gets to play—that's pretty cool."

Although re-enactors certainly do not share homogenous viewpoints on their activities and the messages conveyed, their self-consciousness about their behavior is interesting because it is obvious that in doing so, they feel that they are doing something culturally aberrant. For *Theater of War*, this is extremely important since the events taking place not only involve the usual behaviors of Airsoft play, but also try to re-create historical events with a specific remit—in the words of one of the interviewees, to play a "realistic form" of the paintball matches he had previously taken part in, and also to feel closer to his father (a prior combatant who plays Airsoft, and who supplied him with much of the armor he was wearing).

These representations are also problematic when re-creating wartime scenarios as they raise the troubling issue of "respect"—a term that lurks on the periphery of the interviews and often takes form in statements that express respect for one's peers or the "serious fun" nature of the events themselves. One of the Fresno interviewees describes the participants as "more mature," and also acknowledges the undertones of the events. "Right now it's all fun and games, but this can all be used as knowledge in the future." This respect for the game and its meaning underpins every interview. It is to this issue that the essay now turns.

Mythologies—Reading the theater of war

"Respect" is a hugely codified, emotive term that encompasses several different attitudes: respect for the dead, for the survivors, for historical representation itself, and for the more general ethos that war and its participants should be remembered. This is tempered with the socially accepted view that war is both heroic and hell at the same time. Respect is also an ideological stance—acknowledging that the contemporary participants can never quite realize the conditions of the past, no matter how hard they try.

In his book on the cultural representation of war, historian Samuel Hynes coined a now infamous depiction of these difficult interchanges, which he called "the myth of the war." He described how our understanding of combat is primarily viewed through literary or artistic sources such as novels, films, and poetry, and argues that this skews the representation of warfare into an emotive event, rather than a historical one. Hynes does not deny the events of war, rather he sees the common version of its mythos as: "not a falsification of reality, but an imaginative version of it, the story of the war that has evolved, and has come to be accepted as true" (Hynes 1992: xi). Therefore he describes the myth of World War I thusly:

> A brief sketch of that collective narrative of significance would go something like this: a generation of innocent young men, their heads full of high abstractions like Honour, Glory, and England, went off to war to make the world safe for democracy. They were

slaughtered in stupid battles planned by stupid generals. Those who survived were shocked, disillusioned, and embittered by their war experiences, and saw that their real enemies were not the Germans, but the old men at home who had lied to them. They rejected the values of the society that had sent them to war, and in doing so separated their own generation from the past and from their cultural inheritance.

(Hynes xii)

Hynes' depiction has proven to be extremely useful since it reconfigures war as an ideology, rather than an event. It recognizes that the intention to portray warfare is laced with social and political baggage that influences its representation, and it also acknowledges that we are selective in these representations. The myth helps to explain the difficult relationship between warfare itself, and the cultural ideologies that surround it and may change in line with current, rather than past historical change. This includes, for example, the choice of narrative in videogames, or the portrayal of certain events and behaviors from warfare itself, such as re-enacting Nazis or deciding to exclude certain disturbing elements from re-creations of the war environment.

Theater of War challenges this. The images deliberately highlight the fixed, static nature of wartime photography, and encourage the viewer to consider their falseness. At the same time, the Airsofters themselves directly challenge mythologies of warfare by trying to re-enact them. Airsoft is a unique experience—every event is different. It belies the homogenous nature of an account or poem, since it involves multiple participants, all with different motivations. It focuses on the immediate experience of the soldier and the practicalities of warfare, rather than trying to create a grand ideology. Finally, the closed nature of Airsoft events means that mythologies may be held by individual participants, but the events themselves are not intended to assert a narrative of war outside of the Airsoft space.

Physicalities—Aches where my aches used to be

The myth of the war allows us to understand why certain vistas of war are enforced or excluded in videogames. Games whose ludic objectives are to work as a team and destroy the opposition through violence and military tactics are at odds with the "War is Hell" ideology. Even if we read the kill quotes in *Call of Duty 4*,[2] extorting us to be anti-war, avoid fighting and consider the implication of our actions, at heart we are still playing a fun, challenging game where the object is to shoot and kill the enemy team. The most obvious exclusion, however, is the relationship with videogames and the body.

The fixation with the body is intrinsically linked to war studies, as well as videogame theory. Paul Fussell discusses the semantic implications of "high diction," the words used to make war acceptable. In these, "a wound" becomes honorable and a sign of one's manliness, removing all physical implications except that of increased sexual prowess (1975). The obsession with the wound can be seen throughout war literature, from the work of Joanna Bourke (1996) to recent studies on the work of Frans Kafka by Will Self (2012). The wound and its subsequent release in death are so intensely problematic to us that they run through war literature, and the representation of the body within gaming, sports, and martial activities is hugely affected by this.

As I have argued previously (MacCallum-Stewart 2012), in most games the visceral nature of the body is problematized. The hero of the piece must be more resistant to harm than a human body, capable of sustaining many wounds, attacks, or gunshots before meeting their end. The enemy is ludically weaker, stronger, faster, or cleverer according to archetype. For example, a sniper is usually physically weak, but more difficult to hit, a soldier carrying a Gatling gun is slower than his counterparts, but does more damage, and so on and so forth. When killed, these bodies often linger for scant moments (although this is starting to change as home computers become more powerful) before gradually disappearing by melting, dissolving, or simply vanishing from sight. There is a direct linkage with Fussell's high diction here. His linkage of dead bodies with "dust, or ashes" directly parallels the way that the dead slowly depixelate from our view. Death and the body are handled very differently in games, and often absolve the player from fully appreciating the consequences of their actions. A specific name ("hardcore") exists for games in which the player can only die once without being allowed to continue. More often, players are restored after death to "checkpoints," "spawns," or "save points," terms which are semiotically rich as signifiers in themselves. Because the object of the game is usually to progress through it by either killing all of the opposing team, reaching the end of the level, or defeating all of the opponents through guile or brute force, it is not in the game's interest to dissuade players from doing so. Another component comes from games like *Halo*, *Mass Effect*, or *Assassins Creed* in which the action is displaced—in space, the future, or the imaginative past—to avoid the implications of killing within a historical context.

For the participants in LARP, Airsoft, or *Theater of War*, it is the normality of the body that garners such attention. Often, these people are not soldiers and specifically identify themselves as such. They are not at the peak of physical fitness, although they may use their hobbies as exercise. However it is the physicality of their own bodies that they often return to, counterpoising the inhuman attributes of the videogame character and the idealized representation of the soldier or LARP character to their own abilities. Participants share their "wounds" with pride, often celebrating their abilities to perform above and beyond. While I listen to Participant 6 praise his son's capacity to get "muddy" and "cold," and to work for three hours building the Worth site before the game can be played, my Facebook feed is full of players recounting their experiences of the last weekend's LARP event. An agoraphobic friend is celebrating her ability to get out, "On a happier note, thank you to everyone who made this weekend awesome. My aches have aches and I'm pretty sure I could sleep for a week, but this can only be a good thing. (If nothing else, training for Myths!)," while another is being commiserated for breaking his collarbone. Participant 6, in his interview, discusses the reality of soldiering, and of being a tribesman during a historical re-enactment in physical terms, "Your leg may hurt when you kneel on the ground when the American solider tells you to, it might not feel good. You might have to go to the bathroom. These are real pressures." These events encourage the heroic and the impossible, but are counterpoised by the reality of the human body, and its ability to break easily.

Pleasantries—"No Joke"

> *War! Never been so much fun!*
> *War! Never been so much fun!*
> *Go up to your brother, kill him with your gun,*
> *Leave him lying in his uniform, dying in the sun.*
>
> (Opening music for Cannon Fodder, 1995)

It is unlikely, given the nature of LARP and Airsoft events, that the encounters recorded in the *Theater of War* images are always created and received entirely within the mythologies of reverence and respect. Many of the images are deliberately posed, whereas others—for example, the Airsoft players cheering from the moving vehicle in the Lionclaws series of images—are clearly more spontaneous. Events of this nature celebrate community and cohesiveness as much as they do the representation of warfare. It is also entirely possible that events are understood differently, or are reacted to in unforeseen ways.

In *Wargames: Inside the World of Twentieth Century War Re-enactors*, author Jenny Thompson discusses her unease with military re-creations, especially the portrayal and adoption of Nazi personas (Thompson 2004). It is this aspect of re-enactment that often attracts criticism, and can be used as a site of controversy by both other participants and the media. Re-enactment of Nazi personas or units is illegal in Germany and Austria (as are videogames featuring visual depictions of the Swastika or Adolf Hitler). In 2010, photographs of the Republican candidate for Ohio, Rich Iott, who was a member of a Nazi re-enactment group for several years prior to running for candidacy, were widely circulated to considerable censure (Green 2010). The re-creation and wearing of Nazi uniforms is regarded as epitomizing the problematic responses to REN, and also highlights the conundrums that it presents. Do these representations glorify the Nazi regime or should they have an equal role in accurate historical representations of warfare? Do the participants do so with an awareness of the Nazis that is socially appropriate, or do their personal political beliefs coincide? These subtexts cause difficulties as in many respects they are unanswerable. Hiding Nazis from the theatre of war is often seen to be as inappropriate as representing them, yet the acts that re-enactors must carry out in order to accurately represent them even when simply wearing the uniform (the Nazi salute, goose-stepping, the use of the Swastika) are highly offensive. The representation of the Nazi in REN events is often cited as a point where bleed (and causality) are eschewed in favor of "belief." It also helps to explain why Airsoft groups are often so closed. Events or actions can be easily misinterpreted, and there is also an undeniable connection in many games with militancy and violence that is unsettling. To avoid this conclusion is equally as naïve as the dismissal of more unsettling moments within events, which include personal actions and often laughter.

Somewhat unnerving, it is often humor that allows these re-creations to assume reality. We use humor to offset our understanding of the traumatic, expressing our fear and relief that we have not experienced it ourselves (Freud 1905), and through Fridja's "paradoxical laughter" (1986) whereby we laugh at an inappropriate source. Tendentious or offensive jokes, as Freud recognizes, are often a natural part of humor in which the participants displace aberrant ideas into the realm of comedy. Events of high tension often provoke this laughter, especially when the expected trauma does not occur, and finally, a shared smile or wry aside, especially if it is socially inappropriate, can help us recover our sense of self when confronted with a traumatic event or when the expected event is disconfirmed. More disturbingly however, laughter can also signal complicity and acceptance, and a sociopathic reading suggests that laughter signifies that participants take pleasure from the re-enactment of cruelty and death. The viewer is in this respect reminded of the photographs of Abu Ghraib, in which obscene acts performed on prisoners were photographed for entertainment rather than horror.

Thus, while the *Theater of War* photographs are disturbing, there is also something ludicrous in the placement of people, the deliberate reforming of the image, and the sometimes clashing backgrounds or scenarios that surround each member of the group. In LARP and REN, humor is often used to absolve the re-enactment of events such as this, recognizing that the participants themselves would never do such things in a real situation by placing it within the realm of fantasy, or offsetting disgust or fear at the event. This, of course, assumes that the participants are so uncomfortable with the scenarios that they need to alleviate tension by "laughing it off," and have a full understanding of the potential trauma and offense implicit in the event.

"Becoming": Community building through respect

> *The people here ... y'know (puts hand over heart in salute). They know what they are doing; they know what they're doing. (Raises voice slightly and gestures around him) "We're all friends here!"*
>
> (Fresno interviewee on why he plays)

As Sarah Lynne Bowman argues, role-playing games exemplify Victor Turner's conception of *communitas* (2010: 15–16). For Turner, rituals take place in a liminal space or "moment out of time" (1969: 96), which helps to form a sense of belonging among participants. LARP or Airsoft are typical examples of ritualized space because

> ... they fall into the category of ritual at their essence. They provide enactments of epic stories in a communal context, promoting social cohesion and providing an imaginary space of testing and learning for the individuals within a group.
>
> (1969: 15)

This takes place both external to the game, in the form of like-minded clans, events and games where players gather together, and also within the games themselves, which are often predicated around the idea of a close-knit group or groups of individuals. The base narrative of these games involves the formation of factions, clans, or loyal groups of heroes who band together. The familiar refrain "you meet in a tavern" not only provides players with a common starting place, but also provides players to form close social bonds (over an ale). Community forming or re-establishment is usually the first part of any game, with players recounting where they have been or what they have been doing, creating an idea of their personas, and juggling early group dynamics to see where they might fit in.

Forced communitas of this nature is essential to the success of a role-play event as the group needs to establish a shared sense of being. Unlike actual units in an army, Airsoft players, LARPers, and REN participants are "weekend warriors," interacting for very short periods, yet needing to emulate a sense of teamwork and cohesion very quickly. As a result, and even if a character does not appear to fit in, players will often go to extreme lengths to incorporate them as part of the team. This involves socialization techniques, where bleed is deliberately used to tell players not to behave in certain ways by using the game and its rules as an excuse to enforce good behavior in the "real" world (see MacCallum-Stewart 2011, for a more developed discussion of "good" play and socialization codes). Again there are close similarities with the rapid group formation experienced in online wargaming, where groups often come together very quickly and need to work cohesively. Ernest Adams' "Call to Arms" demonstrates just how important creating a positive atmosphere in these games can be, as well as highlighting some of the more negative effects created when temporary gaming communities are not always able to form these bonds (Adams 2012).

A sense of communitas is also important because it directly plays on tropes of heroism, teamwork, and triumph over great odds. The loyal band of brothers fights together to defeat the monsters or bad guys, and that way everyone emerges a hero, as well as has a sense of belonging. Many fantasy events are often situated as either missions, where small groups head out into the wilderness to defeat enemies, or pageants, celebrations, and festivals, where much larger factions gather to plot, scheme, fight, and boast of previous victories. These two types of events promote both communitas and the heroes within, with the latter being very much about retrospective memory: a vital part of experiential consumption (Holbrook and Hirschman 1982). The heroes re-create their experiences in a shared group, and the nature of the event encourages them to exaggerate their deeds. Sections within these events that celebrate storytelling, musical renditions of past events, and shows of skill or prowess are popular, as they also reinforce the cohesiveness of the group, and showcase both the deeds and abilities of the individual. For Airsoft events, photographs, forums, and online/real-life meet-ups help re-create the event posthumously, enforcing the actual event with retrospective re-creations. These re-creations highlight funny, difficult, or community moments that allow the event to become mythologized as a generally positive event, but also to insert the tropes of warfare that give it retrospective, and recognizable, meaning.

In the *Theater of War* images and interviews, there is an obvious sense of communitas, creating a private, shared environment that might not necessarily be understood by those outside the ritual space. This softens the bleed effect within these games as it highlights the need for shared experience among participants, who are seen to be passing along the ideas and sentiments of war with a recognition that they do so within a ritualized space of the "half-real" (Juul 2005). Participant 1 argues that although he doesn't take part in the events because he is usually organizing them or working behind the scenes, he likes to "help people out, guide things along, share any knowledge that might be valuable and just hang out with people that might appreciate … a certain segment of my life that others might not." For him, being able to re-create wartime scenarios akin to those he experienced in combat during Airsoft events is also an expression of the common split between soldiers and the public—soldiers do not wish to recount their experiences because civilians do not understand them; or rather, they do not understand the sentiments that accompany them. Participant 1 supports this in the interview by immediately describing himself as foulmouthed, and that he regards his public persona as "fake"; whereas in the interview he is well dressed, articulate, and polite. His decision to remain in a formal costume, and to present himself so differently from his words, suggests that his "wartime" persona might be different, and difficult, for others to comprehend.

Conclusion

In *The Soldier's Tale* (1998), Samuel Hynes goes back to the cultural construction of the soldier and discusses why their role is so consistently marginalized in cultural representation, despite the impact of writing by combatants throughout the century. He discusses the need for the soldier to place himself "inside" history, and to relate his part of warfare to greater events. At the same time, the soldier believes that those who were there are the only ones who can understand, forming a paradox between the civilian and the combatant that cannot be resolved upon the return to daily life. It is this paradox that *Theater of War* seeks to resolve, coming into contact with games that appear to be real, but are unreservedly false. It is disingenuous to see these re-creations as entirely benign. Created by the conditions of war, the images are shocking because of their mundanity, and also because people want to (sometimes need to) re-create them as a leisure activity; an act which seems counter-intuitive to the hard-hitting, complex nature of the games' content.

The subculture of live-action games, particularly Airsoft events, is an attempt to experience more accurate representations of warfare. These events go some way to dissolving the face of vainglory, still a part of our culture despite so many years of evidence to the contrary, but at the same time they are also a paradox. While exposing the mundane intricacies of war—the three-hour builds before 30 minutes of "play," and the hours spent planning and organizing each event—these events are still enjoyed by thousands of people in the western world. They give players a sense of purpose and enjoyment, and they allow participants to let off steam in a closed environment where the sentiments of warfare can be more easily understood in a civilian context. The participants of these events are hyper-aware of these conditions, however, and this has also resulted in thoughtful portrayals of combat as discussed by some of the participants, and seen in many of the scenarios that they enact.

We also need to remember at this stage in both cultural development and Game Studies that it is okay to use games as a medium to investigate more serious points. Games provide a sphere in which we can examine disturbing situations or events with the realization that we are just playing, and that our experimentation and experience may lead us further to discover things about ourselves, our communities, and our socio-political make-up. The awareness that the Airsoft space is "half-real"—re-creating actual events in the closed "circle" of the game, and containing some, but not all of the elements of actual war—is unsettling, but this is how it is meant to be. *Theater of War* and the participants that continue to take part in games such as this are deliberately placing themselves in an environment where they can examine these issues. The interviews demonstrate the complexity of their responses, including their own understanding of this. They are playing, learning, and, as one of them identifies, "practicing" for the real thing. In addition, although events like these do create a sense of communitas and memory, they are also highly subject to a memorialization process that can go both ways: exaggerating the importance of warfare and also offsetting its more unsettling elements in humor and transference. These issues are key to the overall experience. The participants want to understand the complexities of warfare, as well as the ways in which society reinterprets it differently from the experience "on the ground"; and for them the paradox of such unreal conflict is one of the draws. The physical videogame nature of Airsoft gives them an altogether more practical understanding of war, and allows them to feel more involved with it as a real event. For those who take part, crossover between bleed, reality, and the closed environment is an intrinsic part of play, which allows them to think more deeply about warfare in an active context. •

GLOSSARY

AAA (or triple A) game. A top-end videogame, usually produced by an established development company, with a large accompanying budget. AAA games are expected to sell in high volume (over several million copies worldwide).

Airsoft. Games that take place using Airsoft weapons; a type of weapon that fires small (air-propelled) pellets designed to scatter rather than cause physical harm.

FPS. First Person Shooter. A videogame genre in which players usually see the game from the perspective of the antagonist, witnessing the game through this character's eyes (or sometimes from a camera positive placed slightly behind them).

LARP (sometimes LRP). Live-Action Role-Play. Although LARP has a variety of permutations, it involves the acting out of fantastic scenarios and events. Many LARPs place an emphasis on costume and remaining "in character" throughout each session.

Ludic. This is a contentious phrase to use in Game Studies, but here I take it to mean any systemic part of the game where rules and systems take precedence over narrative events. Hit points systems are an example of ludic play (see Aarseth for a more developed discussion of ludic behavior in *Cybertext, Perspectives on Ergodic Literature*, 1997).

REN. Re-enactment event. During re-enactments, participants dress as historical characters and re-enact real events from the past. Although they may adopt personas, the emphasis is on historical veracity, speech, and behavior rather than fantastic role-play.

Tabletop. A paper-based role-playing game played on a "tabletop"—the most famous example being Gygax and Arneson's *Dungeons & Dragons*. Players usually use dice and paper, role-playing their characters to various degrees depending on the ludicity of the game.

Section or linear. The name given to a portion of a LARP event where characters carry out a specific task or experience a specific event. For example a puzzle section might see a fantasy LARP attempting to break a wizard's curse through cracking codes or solving riddles, and a linear section might be one where they subsequently journeyed forth to slay her minions.

BIBLIOGRAPHY

Adams, Ernest. 2012. "A call to arms for decent men." *The Designers Notebook*. Available at http://www.designersnotebook.com/Columns/115_A_Call_to_Arms/body_115_a_call_to_arms.htm [Accessed 4 April, 2014].

Anon. April 17, 2009. "Iraq War Video Game Branded Crass and Insensitive by Father of Red Cap Killed in Action". *The Daily Mail*. http://www.dailymail.co.uk/news/article-1168235/Iraq-War-video-game-branded-crass-insensitive-father-Red-Cap-killed-action.html. [Accessed April 4, 2014].

Arseth, Espen. 1997. *Perspectives on Ergodic Literature*. Maryland, BA: John Hopkins University Press.

Barrowcliff, Mark. 2008. *The Elfish Gene*. London: Pan Macmillan.

Bourke, Joanna. 1996. *Dismembering the Male: Men's Bodies, Britain and the Great War*.

Chicago: Reaktion Press and University of Chicago Press.

Bowman, Sarah Lynne. 2010. *The Function of Role-Playing Games*. Jefferson: NC McFarland and Co. Inc.

Crawford, Garry. 2011. *Video Gamers*. London: Routledge.

De Lappe, Joseph. 2006. *Dead in Iraq*. http://www.delappe.net/project/dead-in-iraq/ [Accessed April 4, 2014].

De Lappe, Joseph. 2004. The Great Debates. http://www.delappe.net/play/the-great-debates/ [Accessed April 4, 2014].

Draken, Anders. (ed.). 2008–present. *The International Journal of Role-Playing*. Available at http://journalofroleplaying.org/ [Accessed April 4, 2014].

Freud, Sigmund. 1905 (2002). *Jokes and Their Relation to the Unconscious* (trans. S. Henderson). London: Penguin Classics.

Fridja, Nico. 1986. *The Emotions*. Cambridge: Cambridge University Press.

Fussell, Paul. 1975. *The Great War and Modern Memory*. Oxford: Oxford University Press.

Gilsdorf, Ethan. 2009. *Fantasy Freaks and Gaming Geeks: An Epic Quest for Reality among Role Players, Online Gamers and Other Dwellers of Imaginary Realms*. New York: Globe Pequot Press.

Goffman, Erving. 1974. *Frame Analysis: An Essay on the Organization of Experience*. New York: Harper & Row.

Green, Joshua. October 8, 2010. "Why is this GOP house candidate dressed as a Nazi?" In *The Atlantic*. http://www.theatlantic.com/politics/archive/2010/10/why-is-this-gop-house-candidate-dressed-as-a-nazi/64319/ [Accessed April 4, 2014].

Halter, Ed. 2006. *From Sun-Tzu to X-Box. War and Video Games*. New York: Thunder's Mouth Press.

Hansen, Kasper. (ed.). *Playground*. 2011–present. Available at http://playgroundroleplaying magazine.wordpress.com/about/ [Accessed April 4, 2014].

Harviainen, JiiTuomas. 2011. "This year in Larp Academia." Paper given at Solmukohta. Available at http://www.solmukohta.org/index.php/2012/ProgramDocumentation [Accessed April 4, 2014].

Holbrook, Morris and Hirschman, Elizabeth. September, 1982. "The experiential aspects of consumption: Consumer fantasies, feelings and fun." In *Journal of Consumer Research*. Vol. 9. Available at http://www.scribd.com/doc/7316921/Holbrook-Hirschman-1982 [Accessed April 4, 2014].

Huntemann, Nina and Payne, Matthew Thomas. (eds). 2009. *Joystick Soldiers: The Politics of Play in Military Videogames*. London: Routledge.

Huzingha, Johan. 1938 (1955). *Homo Ludens* (trans. John K. Gillespie). New York: Beacon Press.

Hynes, Samuel. 1992. *A War Imagined: The First World War and English Culture*. London: Pimlico.

Hynes, Samuel. 1998. *The Soldier's Tale: Bearing Witness to Modern War*. London: Penguin Books.

Jenkins, Henry. 1992. *Textual Poachers: Television Fans and Participatory Culture*. New York: Routledge.

Juul, Jesper. 2005. *Half Real: Video Games between Real Rules and Fictional Worlds*. Cambridge, MA: MIT Press.

King, Brad and Borland, John. 2003. *Dungeons and Dreamers. The Rise of Computer Game Culture from Geek to Chic*. New York: McGraw-Hill.

Kowert, Rachel and Oldmeadow, Julian. 2011. "The stereotype of online gamers: New characterization or recycled prototype?". Paper presented at DiGRA 2011. Situated Play. Hilversum, Netherlands. Available at http://www.digra.org/dl/db/12168.23066.pdf [Accessed April 4, 2014].

Lieberman, Jessica. 2008. "Traumatic images." In Photographies. Vol. 1. pp. 87–102.

MacCallum-Stewart, Esther. 2011. "Conflict, thought communities and textual appropriation in MMORPGs." In Crawford, Garry, Light, Ben, and Gosling, Victoria (eds), *Online Gaming in Context*. London: Routledge.

MacCallum-Stewart, Esther. 2012. "Play up and play the Game!"—The narrative of war games." In Piette, Adam and Rawlinson, Ben (eds), *The Edinburgh Companion to British and American Twentieth Century War*. Edinburgh: Edinburgh University Press.

McCabe, Joanne. October 19, 2011. "Parents force daughter to have medieval duel as punishment." *Metro Online*. http://www.metro.co.uk/news/879053-parents-forced-daughter-to-have-medieval-duel-as-punishment [Accessed April 4, 2014].

Montola, Markus. 2010. "The positive negative experience in extreme role-playing." Paper given at Nordic DiGRA 2010. Available at http://www.digra.org/dl/db/10343.56524.pdf [Accessed April 4, 2014].

Newman, James. 2008. *Playing with Videogames*. Oxford: Routledge.

Payne, Matthew Thomas. July, 2012. "Marketing military realism in *Call of Duty 4: Modern Warfare*." *Games and Culture*. Vol. 7, #4. Available at http://gac.sagepub.com/content/7/4/305.full.pdf+html [Accessed April 4, 2014].

Salen, Katie and Zimmerman, Eric. 2003. *Rules of Play*. Cambridge, MA: MIT Press.

Sample. December, 2008. "Virtual torture: Videogames and the war on terror." In *Games*

Studies. Vol. 8, #2. Available at http://www.gamestudies.org/0802/articles/sample

Self, Will. 2012. *Kafka's Wound*. http://thespace.lrb.co.uk/ [Accessed 4 April 2014].

Sitwell, Osbert. 1926. *Before the Bombardment*. London: George H. Doran.

Stenros, Jaakko and Montola, Markus. 2011. *Nordic LARP*. Stockholm: Fëa Livia.

Taylor, TL. 2012. *Raising the Stakes*. Massachusetts: MIT Press.

Thompson, Jenny. 2004. *Wargames: Inside the World of Twentieth Century War Re-enactors*. Washington DC: Smithsonian.

Turner, Victor. 1969. *The Ritual Process: Structure and Anti-Structure*. Aldine Degruyter. Available at http://www.unoacademia.ch/webdav/site/developpement/shared/developpement/mdev/soutienauxcours0809/droz_dieu/Turner_Liminality_communitas.pdf [Accessed April 4, 2014].

Waugh, Rob. April 30, 2012. "At least they ARE getting out more: Hilarious YouTube video shows gamers turning the REAL world into gaming hit Skyrim." *The Daily Mail*. Available at http://www.dailymail.co.uk/sciencetech/article-2137458/At-ARE-getting-Hilarious-video-shows-gamers-turning-REAL-world-10-million-selling-game-hit-Skyrim.html [Accessed April 4, 2014].

Waern, Annika. 2010. "'I'm in love with someone that doesn't exist!' Bleed in the context of a computer game." Paper given at Nordic DiGRA 2010. Available at http://www.digra.org/dl/db/10343.00215.pdf [Accessed April 4, 2014].

GAMEOLOGY

America's Army. 2002–present. US Army.

Assassin's Creed II. 2009. [videogame, various systems].

Bigger Guns. 2005. Gregorzck and TTSNB. [LARP].

Call of Duty 4: Modern Warfare. 2007. Infinity ward [videogame, various systems].

Cannon Fodder. 1995. Sensible Software. [Amiga].

Distant Vista. Craig, Roo. 2004–present. [LARP].

Dungeons and Dragons. Arneson, Dave and Gygax, Gary. 1974. [Tabletop RPG].

E-Zero. Rif Airsoft. 2008–present. [LARP/Airsoft].

The Gathering. 1991–present. Lorien Trust. [LARP].

Halo. 2001. Bungie. [videogame, various systems].

Mass Effect. 2007. Bioware. [videogame, various systems].

Minecraft. 2009–present. Mojang Specifications. [videogame, PC].

Six Days in Fallujah. 2009. Atomic Games [unreleased].

ENDNOTES

1   See the glossary for a description of the various terms and unfamiliar phrases used in this essay.

2   Kill quotes are short quotations that appear on the screen when the player has died. In *Call of Duty 4* there are nearly 50, ranging from statistics about the "cost" of warfare to quotes from famous American generals and politicians of the twentieth century. They include "Anyone who truly wants to go to war, has truly never been there before!" (Reeves) and "The real and lasting victories are those of peace, and not of war" (Emerson).

WAR SIMULATION GAMING: SPORTING TRAUMA
Jessica Catherine Lieberman

We humans presume that we experience the world as analog. Our physiology assures us that the world is continuous rather than discrete. However, our scientific understanding of the mechanisms of the human optical system undercuts the assertive force of our physiological experience. While we may understand that our vision is not continuous, that it flickers on and off, we confront a paradox between experiential and theoretical knowledge.

As human experience relies increasingly on computers and computation, we encounter a nostalgia for the analog: such technologies, we assume, precede digital ones and must therefore be more authentic. But these categories, as our own bodies teach us, are inherently unstable and boundaries between them are redefined continually. The analog and the digital are always making and remaking one another.

As discrete fabricators of identity, human subjects rely upon such a dichotomy to enable and authorize a number of ideological assumptions. Whether we are predicting the apocalyptic onslaught of the digital into a humanist world, or isolating the analog/digital divide as the latest sea-change to impact a vulnerable society, debates in the popular press and scholarly venues share a sustained fascination with (a) an inevitable slide into dehumanization and desensitization via digital overstimulation and with (b) the well-rehearsed battle between ontologies of continuity versus fragmentation that discourses of the digital have re-inscribed and been mapped onto.

How does such a modern individual—one for whom both structures of temporal experience play concurrently in the sense of self—function? Theorists of cyberspace debate the negative connotations of "digital dualism,"[1] "the belief that technology creates an alternate, virtual universe that is separate from everyday reality" (Bulajewski 2012). Younger scholars are now positing "augmented reality" as a more appropriate descriptor of human/technology relations: "Today, the reality is that both the digital and the material constantly augment one another to create a social landscape ripe for new ideas" (Jurgenson 2010; Rey 2012). It is within this notion of an *augmented reality* that visual artist Meredith Davenport's subjects are constituted.

|

In Davenport's unsettling project, *Theater of War*, individuals experience such augmentations in playing combat video games, simulating war scenarios, and re-enacting historical battles. The Airsoft gamers that Davenport documents through photographs, interviews, videos, and performance are citizens of both time frames; they move without hesitation or apparent awareness between analog and digital and among virtual gameplay, live-action gameplay, and "reality." Airsoft participants describe the game as a "sport" which uses highly realistic replica firearms that update the classic BB gun in order to participate in orchestrated scenarios (Davenport "interviews"). One player comes to the game in the expensive military costume that he purchased online. Another dons the fatigues that "saw action" on the back of his father on the battlefields of historical war. While these players perform staged scenes with Airsoft rifles in the nearby woods, others—in shorts and t-shirts—play out similar scenarios online in air-conditioned headquarters. Companies across the United States, United Kingdom, Europe, and Asia have arisen to provide gameplay scenarios ranging from simple skirmishes and skill tests to elaborately organized war simulations, historical re-enactments, and fictional military encounters involving historical groups and present-day enemies. Companies such as MindGame Productions and Battlesim.com boast of military-trained staff and veteran expertise in the promise of authentic tactical training and scenario experiences.[2] Specialty retail shops and online stores compete with institutions such as Walmart, offering military uniforms, equipment, and police paraphernalia to supplement their Airsoft firearms and BB ammunition. Lawmakers have seen a need to legislate restrictions at the state and federal levels due to the realism of gameplay weaponry.[3]

The players range from young to old, rich to poor, experienced to inexperienced, hard-core hobbyist to occasional participants. Some are veterans; some have no experience with the military. The clearest demographic factor is gender: these players are decidedly male (a point that I will return to later in this essay). What they share in common, what brings them to the field of wargame play and re-enactment, is an important question. Who are these men who have formed this elaborate subculture and what is it that draws them to play at war? Is it a mere extension of "boys will be boys" narratives into a digital era? Or is it a return from digital gameplay back to analog, backyard re-enactments? These are the questions Davenport explores as she embeds herself, like a war photographer, in this gaming counterculture.

Davenport's approach to these gamers is a careful combination of documentary photojournalism and critical fine art. Concerned with issues of human rights and social justice, Davenport's work has focused on violence, war, aftermath, and the forgotten with the photojournalistic lens of idealistic neutrality. With *Theater of War,* Davenport explores similar issues and concerns, but on very different terrain. Neutral or not, the subjects of her projects for *National Geographic* and *The New York Times Magazine* come with a determined set of values for interpretation: child soldiers in Colombia and pesticide poisoned children in Costa Rica come prepackaged as sympathetic and wronged. This time, the subjects may not be relatable or sympathetic in the traditional ways. A viewer may feel a draw toward the gaming habits of a veteran who has endured the horror of war and the agonies of battle. Such behaviors can be seen as therapeutic or redemptive or professionally practiced. An audience may also understand the use of these simulations for trainees, young soldiers about to enter the battlefield using these experiences to hone technical skills and prepare mentally for imminent deployment. These subjects do appear. But their presence is part and parcel of a larger participation that evokes complicated responses from the viewer. Some players are dismissable or laughable and arouse amusement. Some are disturbing or frightening and provoke disgust. All together, they are a problematic subject group, alternately baiting the viewers, or charming them, or inciting them to action. This is where Davenport brings her critical and artistic eye to her journalistic method. She does not judge her characters, but offers them up to us in earnest fascination.

Key to the mutability of their character, and the uncertain sympathetic aspect of their role, is the figuring of these gamers as survivors and victims on one end, or brutes and "wannabes" on the other. Our responses as viewers are tied to our sense of our subjects as good guys or bad guys, heroes or miscreants. Davenport's presentation does not simply goad the viewer with this uncertainty, however. At the same time, she presents her subjects themselves as enmeshed in the ambiguity of their character. In her video compilations, interviewees reveal dramatic shifts in self-perception. These shifts highlight uncertain spectrums of time, of place, of fantasy, and reality. One young man narrates his near-death experiences in Iraq; his personal reaction to seeing friends get shot and die in explosions; the simulation games he plays, produces, and promotes; scenes from the movie *Apocalypse Now*; and paradigms from the TV show *Star Trek* in one free flowing, continuous whole, moving fluidly, and without awareness between the various levels of reality as if each shares the same authenticity in his experience. Violent death and cinematic end-credits play equivocal roles in framing his perception of his own experience. An angry veteran swings wildly between pride in his military service in distinction from the unimportance of civilian life; annoyance that his service has no value and that "his country" does not know who he is; refusal to serve his country again because he is disrespected; and assurance that he would of course fight if needed because he is not a coward. A company administrator dressed in a suit explains that he does not think people should use guns, and goes on to explain that guns are foundational to American society and that the knowledge to use a gun is a responsibility, like driving a car, and that guns are a way to "hopefully become better" and, for children, "a way to approach problems." A boy dresses up in his veteran father's uniform and equipment from Kuwait, details how each important piece of his borrowed costume was authentically worn in the service, and explains that he attends these games because they are not real and he wants to follow in his father's footsteps (Participant 1 2006; Participant 3 2006; Participant 5 2007; Participant 6 2007; Participant 4 2006; Participant 7 2007).

These fluid, shifting, and contradictory expressions of self, desire, and experience are played out in a multi-platform, multidimensional community of fantasy role-playing with extreme violence, real-world, historical tragedy, and real-world, unresolved distress. Confused but passionate boys and men perform their uncertainty and angst in elaborately staged scenarios while seeking a kind of legitimacy, authenticity, and real-life respectability that is undermined even as they stage its derivation. They are, at the same time, survivors and casualties, victims and heroes, who pretend in order to instantiate a real life. In search of this longed-for, authentic "experience," gamers use virtual-analog play and virtual-digital play as coterminous strategies. Wargaming companies provide combinations of online forums, in-house PC arrays for multi-player shooter games to be played by fellow gamers in one another's company, and live-action Airsoft "events." Battlesim.com, which focuses on battle simulations, provides "training" and "rehearsal" before "events" and "debriefing" and follow-up "coaching" after. "In order to make our simulations more 'real,'" their website explains, "we have a strong commitment to training. Our feeling is that players make the events… We want you to feel as if you are in the trenches!… you might 'forget' for a moment you are playing a game is the whole reason we do this." Operations have a "'Hollywood' aspect to them" but with "more depth and realism than a movie could provide." Battlesim.com concludes, "It's about the experience."

The terms "reality" and "experience" recur with regularity in the literature of the various companies, who promise experiences that are *more real* by means of *virtual* augmentation and simulation. It would be easy to dismiss these games as Debordian spectacle, decrying that, lived experience has been sacrificed to a world of mere representation. Guy Debord's 1967 *The Society of the Spectacle* is indeed a preemptive critique on virtual reality. Attacking what he sees as the "weakness" of the western philosophical project, the spectacle follows in the misguided attempt to understand experience within categories of the visual:

> In societies dominated by modern conditions of production, life is presented as an immense accumulation of *spectacles*. Everything that was directly lived has receded into a representation… The images detached from every aspect of life merge into a common stream in which the unity of that life can no longer be recovered. *Fragmented* views of reality regroup themselves into a new unity as a *separate pseudoworld* that can only be looked at… The spectacle is a concrete inversion of life… real life is materially invaded by the contemplation of the spectacle, and ends up absorbing it and aligning itself with it. The spectacle presents itself… as a *means of unification*… it is in reality the domain of delusion and false consciousness: the unification it achieves is nothing but an official language of universal separation.
>
> (Debord: 1–3)

Debord's disgust is for the false consciousness that overtakes lived experience when the fragmented spectacle of the virtual era debases the unity of analog life. It is specifically the technologies developed in the service of the visual, imaging technologies that take the revolutionary character out of life and leave individuals enslaved to the ideological progression of the simulacra. Debord joins Jean Baudrillard, another seminal social theorist and critic, in querying the "hyperreality" of a world in which individuals are drawn to "simulations." Baudrillard, however, dismisses the notion of a "reality" that we could return to outside of the "simulacra"; all experience is of simulation.

Though Davenport's gamers may not be familiar with the theoretical arguments of Debord and Baudrillard, they are, in their own way, "in on the joke" of the metaphysical pining for idealized reality and experience. As the young son dressed in his father's military uniform explains, "this is not real and I don't want to sound crazy but ….you know just give me some kind of experience." In an important way, these foundational discourses are inadequate in accounting for these gamers. These players take on history and fantasy, fact and fiction, as a performative sport. Debord argues that false consciousness is born of a repression, "imposed at every moment of everyday life subjected to the spectacle—a subjection that systematically destroys the "faculty of encounter" and replaces it with a *social hallucination: a false consciousness of encounter, an "illusion of encounter."* In a society where no one can any longer be *recognized* by others, each individual becomes incapable of recognizing his own reality" (217). The repression vilified by Debord, Baudrillard, and the many others of the Marxist and semiotic schools is inadequate to account for the present-day psyche and its relationship to experience. Their presumption of a society constituted through social hallucination is based in a digital dualism, a false dichotomy that requires these theorists to posit the individual as one who cannot discern between physical and virtual aspects of their larger experience. By such a dualist logic, individuals are victims, existentially damaged by the therapeutic aims of repression as their psyches' encounter increasing levels of media. As in its careful documentation and representation of these modern-day gamers, Davenport's *Theater of War* calls for a shift in this discourse, for a post-psychoanalytic narrative of the functioning of repression in the formation of a modern, augmented self.

II

When Freud first laid out his model of the psyche, repression played an important defensive role, figuring as a self-protective mechanism that could filter out experiences that it did not want to internalize. The double-edge on that sword was the potentially damaging effects of the filtering itself. Though inhibited, the experience nonetheless took place, and its latent affect—repressed away by the mind—might cause a damage of its own. Debordian repression is more existential than psychic: his concern is not with the potential dangers to an individual mind but with the false consciousness experienced by a society at large when the very act of experience itself, the faculty of encounter, has been so damaged by repeated repression that it no longer functions in reality but is enslaved to illusion. The schism that animates this dialectic today is the analog/digital divide, the digital dualism discussed earlier in this essay. Our current stage of simulacra, whether stimulated by augmented reality or under its siege, is played out in dramatic form by the Airsoft gamers who not only traverse its technical landscapes, but also its psychic minefields. For the "games" these players seek out are premised on our most loaded, most disturbing, most devastating sets of human experience. In the United States, for example, staged conflicts include the hunt for Osama bin Laden and showdown with Raul Castro. These battles are played with "enemy" actors wearing World War II uniforms alongside players in contemporary Arabic garb, blending the "bad guys" of past and present into an amalgamation of evil. In important ways, the scenario itself, with all the emphasis on its accuracy, need only be accurate to the player's sense of historical trauma, not historical detail. The enemies must be the perceived boogeymen of communism, Nazism, fascism, or terrorism, the evil-doers that threaten our sense of safety, autonomy, or freedom and they should be engaged in a setting that fits our perception of territories threatened or in need of liberation.

The re-enactments are, crucially, re-enactments of shared social traumas, not historical events. The authenticity of the scenario must live up to the sense of threat, of terror, of confusion, and adrenaline. It need not match details of history, but must match details of associative fear. The game, the sport, the engagement is of trauma. This is not a revelation. Indeed, it is this play-with-psychic-pain aspect of the game that exposes the players to legal, social, scholarly, and artistic scrutiny. We are not shocked by Civil War re-enactments and their focus on historical war. Nor do we focus our concern on the video games in which first-person shooters violently murder nonhuman foes. It is not the subject matter of history or the behavior of violence that troubles us here. It is the engagement with, and further the play with, trauma.

In "Traumatic Images," I posited the pathology of trauma as a useful framework for thinking about the effect and affect of images on viewers (Lieberman 2008). Linking the arguments of trauma theorists Sigmund Freud, Cathy Caruth, and Ruth Leys to the photographic criticism and philosophy of Roland Barthes, Susan Sontag, and Vilém Flusser, I showed how trauma is a useful critical category for understanding structures of reception and human experience. Trauma is key to our discussion here. Not only is trauma part of a practical aspect of the simulated wargaming performed by Davenport's boys and men, but trauma also illuminates the contemporary reality of these players for whom the real/false dichotomy is irrelevant in terms of human experience. Through their trauma play, these gamers dispel myths of digital dualism and spectacle.

In her seminal discussions of trauma, Cathy Caruth explains that the emphasis in a trauma is on the *structure of its experience* (Caruth 1995: 4). When the precipitating "event" occurs, it is received in such a way that it is not fully assimilated by the psyche. Instead, the psyche defers the experience, delaying its reception as a protective mechanism. The psyche defends itself from "reality," distancing itself from unwanted events by means of a time shift. Caruth explains, "Trauma is not experienced as a mere repression or defense, but as a temporal delay that carries the individual beyond the shock of the first moment. The trauma is a repeated suffering of the event, but it is also a continual leaving of its site" (Caruth: 10). The downside, so to speak, in this belated experience, is that the protection of the psyche in the present moment leads to disturbances in the future. As the current explosion of cases of "post-traumatic stress disorder (PTSD)" in military personnel returning from Afghanistan and Iraq highlights, PTSD may be the most disabling legacy of this century's response to terrorism (Zoroya 2011; *NIH Medline Plus* 2009; *Psychology & Psychiatry* 2012).

A number of points here are crucial to our discussion. The trauma at issue is not an event alone; it is not a blow or an act. It is, rather, a mode of experience, a structure of reception, or as Debord might understand it, a "faculty of encounter." It is the way in which the event comes to impact an individual. This mode or structure is notable in its aim—a protective deferral—and its method—a temporal dislocation. With trauma, the experience is not magically transcended, nor is it repressed into avoidance. It is indeed experienced by the individual, but later, in a different time, and thus in a different space. The protection from the shock of the moment comes at the cost of a future commitment. Furthermore, this future commitment has an additional time-component: one of repetition. In dislocating the event from its origin, the traumatic deferral has liberated the event from context and unleashed it on the psyche unfixed—it can return to do damage in unimagined ways and at unexpected times. Anxiety disorders that result from the trauma are not the same as the trauma, and this distinction is important. My argument here is based on the pathology, or structuring, of trauma as a critical category for investigation. It is not intended to speak to the vital and urgent work being done on PTSD diagnosis and treatment.

Traumatic time is a deferral that results in a recurring present, an echo. Traumatic events, it follows, function for the psyche in their remembering, reliving, or belated return. The original event is important as a trigger, but in the pathways of trauma, that event qua experience, never really happened. The echo is the experience. Traumatic reality, finally, becomes one of highly internalized responses; both time and space have shifted and the real experiences that the individual must survive are happening outside of the "real" phenomenon. A trauma-based conception of experience, then, would not concern itself with the true/false, authentic/virtual schisms of reality in a binary way. As I have argued, the relationship between reality and the way it is interpreted is supposed to be altered in trauma; the modes of memory and forgetting are not expected to fulfill an ideal of accuracy. Furthermore, a recurring traumatic present—historically unfixed—recognizes a latency in experience. Freud and Caruth describe an important aspect of traumatic experience: that the original event is not forgotten, but that it is never fully experienced in the first place, "an inherent latency within the experience itself… it is only in and through its inherent forgetting that it is first experienced at all" (Caruth: 8). It is this latency in experience, the understanding of reality through the lens of trauma, that captures the seemingly enigmatic interest in wargaming. Not only do these players make sport of historical traumas, but the structuring of their sport functions in a trauma register. It does not matter that the skirmishes be "real;" it does not matter if the enemy threat is authentic. What matters is that the experience sought after, the connection, or shared, communal involvement, is enacted in the space of the game.

In the traumatic register, the veteran who has seen action and the son who was back home in diapers at the time can have similarly ambivalent reactions to the historical events that initiate a trauma and condemn individuals to constantly relive it. Just as the latency in an event means that for any given individual the event never happened, so too does this allow for the traumatized reactions of those who "were not there." The notion of a United States public who can experience the events of 9/11 as a "national trauma" depends on the latent threat of terror as an experience, not on the actuality of a plane impacting a building.

How then does the gaming function in this traumatic register? Trauma diagnosis is built on the recognition of symptoms caused by the revisiting of the site of initial (non)experience. This is the perpetual haunting of the traumatized individual by the deferred event. Again, the event is not magically avoided. It is temporally delayed by the psyche, dislodged from the expectations of linear, continuous time, and launched into a future range in which it does not fit, and so impacts sporadically and unexpectedly. On boutique and corporate websites, wargamers are promised the experience that they missed, real battle action, by means of a variety of revisitations. It is not simply the live-action play made available; rather, it is the training, rehearsal, debriefing, follow-up coaching, and general community acceptance that round out the experience. Though the bombastic claims include the goal that "you might 'forget' for a moment you are playing a game," the gamers who perform for Davenport's lens are not in search of false consciousness. In interview after interview, players and administrators reference the community of other players as the highlight, the experience of a constructed reality together that matters. More apt then, perhaps, is the website claim: "Our feeling is that players make the events" (http://www.battlesim.com/different.html).

Rethinking experience as based on a traumatic structure need not diminish other critically relevant dimensions of inquiry. It is not an exclusive approach. Certainly, these gamers are dealing with trauma: reconstructing events that were traumatic for themselves or for others. Whether this dealing is an evasion or an engagement is varied and debatable. What is expansive here is the way in which trauma's spatial and temporal distinctions discussed above illuminate the "play" in these games. First, there is its spatial relativity. As with trauma, the re-enactors mode is, by definition, a re-spacing of events. Second and third are the two temporal aspects of trauma. An experience that would have occurred and then registered as past is here restaged as a recurring present with each new enactment. Thus, the dislocated experience is both delayed and repeated, as gamers train for, enact, and debrief on events that took place in other times, spaces, and fantasies. It is in the space of Caruth's "inherent latency" in the experience itself that these gamers "play" and perform. As opened in the trauma register, then, the gamer experience is not restricted to a linear, historical model or even to one of "authentic" experience. Theoretically, inherent latency might open out to a freedom for play and imagination for a generation of gamers encountering an augmented reality. Trauma need not only exemplify Debord's damage to our faculties of encounter, but may recognize the play of encounter when responding to the inherent latency in reality.

Davenport's imaging of these players, and her reconstruction of her own set of events by means of artistic performance, calls attention to the temporal aspect of the traumatic visitations as well as the broader connection between trauma and photography that I have outlined elsewhere:

> …there is an analogy between the structure of meaning in trauma and the structure of meaning in photography. Just as the trauma originates in an absence or non-experience, so too does a photograph. The meaning of the photograph lies not in the original event, but in its subsequent reception and perpetual re-interpretation. There is, in effect, no original event or experience in the relevant sense… The photograph that confronts a viewer may or may not reference a moment that was experienced by a subject. Irrespective of whether the recorded instant is posed, falsified, manipulated or a straightforward, realist capture, the representational product delivers an experience that may never have registered in a subject's own psyche. The mechanical record cannot attest to an existentially incorporated real.
>
> (Lieberman 2008: 89)

If I view a photograph of woman giving birth in 1892, I am not experiencing childbirth, nor am I experiencing life in her world in 1892. The original reality is so deferred by the image that it might be functionally irrelevant to me as a viewer. What is relevant, however, is my belated experience of the indexed event *as an image*. Davenport's photographs add yet another layer to the self-referential, frame-within-a-frame aspect to re-enactment. The players chase new experience by reliving a past, dramatizing the simulated aspect of experience itself. Davenport furthers the deferral, imaging the recreations for yet another set of players, a photographic audience.

Davenport emphasizes the latency in this traumatic sport through her reference to iconic imagery and her reactivation of her photographs back into performance. Gamers construct the scenarios based on famous images made by witnesses who were present historically. Then, they document their re-enactments and post video and still images online for further consumption by the community. Davenport speaks to this referentiality and photographs the gamers with an eye to her own photojournalistic forebears, capturing players as they stage poses such as Luc Delahaye's 2001 "Taliban." Thus it is the history of interpretations of a photograph that is sought, not any ur-reality to be regained. This photographic gaming suggests the limits of Susan Sontag's famous assertion about the inseparability of war and photography: "The feeling of being exempt from calamity stimulates interest in looking at painful pictures, and looking at them suggests and strengthens the feeling that one is exempt" (Sontag 1990: 168). Neither the gamers, nor Davenport herself, are seeking exemption. As re-enactors, they are inserting themselves into the process and as gamers; they are implicating themselves in the performance of interpretation. Players may well come to the game in search of exemption from traumatic effect. The staging of battle certainly provides a "safe" environment for role-playing and fantasy, without the messy dangers of physical injury and death. When Participant 3 explains that an attraction to the games is that, "You're not gonna die," he does so from the mixed perspective of a violent combat gamer and as a manager in a business, manipulating the ambivalent desires for violence and security that war and wargaming engage (Participant 3 2006). It is Davenport's viewers, furthermore, who are provoked by the nagging knowledge that whatever societal calamity these boys represent, it is a highly complicated one and one in which we may well be complicit.

Further teasing out this complex string of exemption and complicity in the viewing of photographs, Davenport stages performances that re-enact the photographs she has made of gamers re-enacting iconic imagery. Davenport places live actors in the gallery space, in front of large-scale photographs that have been stripped of their human characters, and directs the actors to perform as the soldier/gamers who have been removed. The gallery viewer experiences a re-enactment in the living present, watching as the performer stages not the original event, nor even the re-enacted event, but rather the *imaged* event, in all its static, two-dimensionality. These performances draw out a number of critical inquiries. Challenging Sontag's concern, the performances call upon the ways in which simulations do not simply protect us from trauma, but can produce new forms of trauma on their own. New technologies—once photography now digital gaming—can bring trauma even closer, bringing distant viewers into close proximity to crisis. The mediation of imaging and virtual technologies is not protective when it puts us face-to-face with demons we would never have witnessed. Instead of distancing tools, or deferrals, these augmentations to reality can just as readily serve as purveyors of proximity. The deployment of unmanned drones, for example, is seen as a means to protect soldiers from the physical dangers of engagement, but the soldier at the flight console is exposed to a whole new set of traumatic experience. Now she makes life and death choices five inches away from her face on a screen that puts her in immediate proximity to geographically distant enemies and renders her actions effective on a plane of intangible reality. Her experience is not analog, per se, but it is a digital experience making an analog one for her; she knows that the images on her screen are not real, but her actions and their consequences are. Again, the latency of the event, mediated through new technologies, leaves the individual psyche wrestling with a traumatic reality.

These spatial-temporal shifts fuel the persistent anxieties that accompany our relationship to emerging technologies. Just as Jurgenson and Rey promote the value of a notion of augmented reality today, defenders of photography such as Vilém Flusser and Ulrich Baer stressed the value of photography's nonsequential capture of bursts of experience and its resistance of the linear model of continuous history (Flusser 2000; Baer 2002). In a way, the wargames played by these citizens of an augmented reality are re-sequencings of the past in an attempt to make fuller sense of the present. The historical reality of Hitler or Castro or bin Laden's social and cultural circumstances are sublimated to the more relevant situation of the gamer's fears and beliefs, and the game provides a space to perform that anxiety. Does this mean, then, that the gaming is therapeutic? And if it is, is it therapeutic in a disturbing way, satisfying uninformed fears at the expense of education? There may well be therapeutic benefit to revisiting scenes of traumatic events for veterans in search of ways to "master" their disruptive pasts. Re-enactments are a treatment method for trauma used in psychotherapy (Levy 2008). Perhaps, then, others who are traumatized by war, irrespective of their own presence at a battle, might benefit from integrating these events into their experience to more fully be able to cope with their own reactions to it. A further stretch could allow for re-enactment as a strategy for facing the imagined terrors that intrude on any psyche, an "attempt to achieve mastery" (Levy 2008) over the numbing or anxiety-provoking realities of everyday life by means of practiced, adaptive mechanisms. Whether or not the gaming is a healing act, it is a performance not just of events, but also of a construction of self.

Where Michel Foucault's concept of "regulative discourses" and Judith Butler's notion of "gender performativity" coerce subjects to perform their identities based on unseen ideological influences, Davenport's gamers speak of a civilian society that does not understand them and forces them to conform to practices which do not accurately represent them. Interviewees speak of the need to "put on" events that draw a community of players to whom they can relate more authentically. Veteran and event coordinator Participant 1 explains that the gaming community, "appreciate a certain segment of my life that some of my other friends may not appreciate…that for me, that's probably what it is" (p. 68 of this volume). He returned from war not speaking a language that civilians could relate to. His stories would shock. He found stories of "death and killing" to be funny and thought that joking about it proved he was "level-headed": "The last thing I'd want to do is look stupid…there were stories that I think are appropriate to tell about my previous lives… years at war… that are not appropriate to tell people, that like really freaks other people out." The game provides not just a community of like minds, but a community that specifically games the very possibility of trauma: "Nothing really brings people together like the threat of imminent and horrible death" (p. 68 of this volume). The goal is not to forget reality or to forge an alternative fantasy. The game is not separate from the real in any meaningful way. The goal is in redefining the rules of reality, in defining a real in which experience is constructed in and through the imaginative and performative choices of each individual gamer and the larger gaming society.

In the American forum, this desire to create a reality that better fits a sense of a lost, idealized past functions in a particularly libertarian register. Ideals of freedom and liberty recur with frequency, and players repeatedly assert their right to do what they want so long as nobody is harmed. Jason Daniel argues that the games teach decision-making skills, methods for approaching problems, and teamwork. He explains, "There is no one who has control over you and no one can make you do anything that you don't want to do…all the ugly nasty parts… of being in the army, you know, is what we take out… leave people making annoying stupid governmental decisions that completely screw up your life… because of red tape… we take the bureaucracy out of it I guess and just we kind of leave the fun" (p. 69 of this volume). Following Participant 3's claims, players presume there are no deep psychic consequences or cumulative ideological effects to their gaming. Their acts of war were acts of choice, voluntary and controlled. On this line of thought, the purpose of the game could be to repress the very possibility of trauma by replacing the potential of uncertainty with intentional experience. The more a player intensifies the role of play, the greater the intensification of denial and the more the player can bypass the consequence of trauma. Play and trauma are secretly if unconsciously linked in their psychic processing. Perhaps gaming and trauma share a pathology, as the intensification of experience sought is an intensification of the denial that play and trauma bear on any relationship.

Notably then, these libertarian principles are played out in a commercially orchestrated production. This is a widely distributed entertainment industry organized around relating wargames and engaging in denial of trauma. As a visual economy, the games are infinitely circulate-able and editable, providing a play-realm for trauma that is codified and determined while seeming emancipatory and open-ended. This leads to a broader, ontological question: what does it mean to have these games imaged, made visible, and consumed? Does this mediation distance us further from recognizing our psychic involvement? Players perform these immersive games with cameras strapped to their heads, providing for screen-within-screen alternative viewpoints when replaying their experiences online later.[4] Once the event is posted as a digital artifact, one need not worry about the real, because it can be infinitely remediated. Appropriated through the visual and focused into this one modality of visibility, one can avoid all other layers of experience, sensory and psychic.

III

Broader questions of visual economy, circulation, and consumption are played out further against a backdrop of social and political realities. Despite the diversity of players noted earlier, it is nonetheless a very particular group of people who are most vulnerable to and enthusiastic about this kind of experience. Gender and class preferences are joined by categories of previous experience, such as dispositions to violence. Participant 3 admits that his clientele look like "a bunch of white guys with guns," and notes that many find it unappealing because it is so "militaristic." One player explains that some of the best infantrymen are hunters: "Cover. Concealment. Camouflage…some of the best hunters of men are hunters of animals." A game administrator defends Airsoft by stating, that "The world is getting more dangerous… things that we thought were isolated to other countries and bad places in the world and dark corners, they're creeping up here."

Women are notably missing from the community. The lone appearance of women in the online forums is in promotional videos for Lion Claws—which bills itself as "the largest professionally operated Airsoft tactical military simulation in North America"—in which the "Angel Team" of women wish the organization a happy anniversary and pose seductively for a camera in heavy makeup (Lion Claws and "About the Angel Team" 2011). A male organizer explains that a lone female employee of his organization became known as the "hot camera chick" and he realized the opportunity to market "beautiful women who are willing to go out there, carry that backpack, carry that gun, break their nails, sweat, climb that hill, and then take you out… that is hot." He admits that they do not attend many events and that they are "actors" rather than players. Davenport draws attention to the gendered affinity for wargame play in her performance pieces, casting a gender-ambiguous actor in the role of a lone soldier and calling attention to the unexpectedly feminized or youthful aspect of a soldier singled out and alone. Davenport also presents interviewee Participant 3 as he explains that the longer he is away at work, the happier his wife is, as "she'll get to clean more of the living room." The gendered feedback loop is tight and the machismo of participation self-selects women out of the game world. The games not only call for a gendered participation but also shape an understanding of what kind of body is necessary for play.

Davenport is joined by fellow contemporary artists Suzanne Opton and Wafaa Bilal in emphasizing the political and performative dimensions of war and identity-construction. Opton's photographic project "Soldier," a series of portraits shown in 2006 and 2007 and then launched as billboards displayed from 2008 to 2010, documents soldiers and veterans of Iraq and Afghanistan.[5] The disconcerting portraits show only large, disembodied, and decontextualized heads lying on a hard table, facing sideways. The extreme close-up provides striking intimacy and proximity to the intense detail on the young faces. If not for the title of the images, and perhaps the haircuts, there is no other information to anchor these floating faces. Many of the faces seem distant, numbed, stunned, or distracted. In an interview with Jim Casper, Opton explains, "Some of them look serene and some of them look shell-shocked… They're all terribly vulnerable." Viewer response, Casper concludes, is to feel "forced into an uncomfortably intimate proximity with someone who appears to be traumatized. It is hard to shake that feeling" (Casper 2008).

Unlike Davenport's process, in which she embeds herself into the action and directly interviews and captures photographs of intentional performances by her subjects, Opton's process deploys performance toward a different end, staging her actions as a photographer to capture her subjects in distracted moments of unguarded vulnerability. In effect, Opton stages a performance of the act of image-making—creating a contextless environment in the studio to highlight the everyman character of each soldier-subject. Under the carefully crafted circumstances, the soldiers are not only self-aware and uncomfortable, but also become detached and distracted as the photographer goes about her business in silence. As their minds wander, they develop a range of facial expressions that Opton can document and recontextualize into an artistic vision of trauma: "I think of this a little bit as performance art…I wanted to make them kind of theatrical because I think there's a certain kind of glamour to the military and the way it presents and sells itself… Studio pictures are abstracted from life, extracted from a sense of place so the color and light was meant to imply a sense of place. If they were fallen where would they be?" (Moakley 2011). Opton performs for her photographic subject and then stages the photographs as performances for the viewer. The point is to challenge the audience: "We are inured to pictures of war," she says. "This may have more power than a documentary picture. It makes you think. It's a conceptual photo based on a documentary situation and that's what I'm interested in" (Moakley 2011).

Thus, whereas Davenport documents "everyman" citizens as they stage themselves as soldiers, Opton restages her soldiers as "everyman" figures of trauma. Both artists approach their subjects with respect while critiquing the horror of their circumstances through a play of photography and performance. Each deploys the photograph in search of the "theater" of war—the performative aspect of individual and communal identity-construction in the face of extreme and shocking violence. Their projects illuminate Judith Butler's "frames" of war, "the ways of selectively carving up experience as essential to the conduct of war" (Butler 2010: 26). Crucially, these frames "do not merely reflect on the material conditions of war, but are essential to the perpetually crafted *animus* of that material reality" (Butler 2010: 26). For both artists, it is this perpetual crafting of animus which they seek to present to viewers. "Soldier" aims to put the viewer face-to-face with the trauma that might be a soldier's experience: "It's about looking at these guys and wondering what they went through.[6] How would they continue with their lives, with something that's never going to go away—how do you manage your life around that?" (Moakley 2011). In interviews, Davenport's players articulate concerns similar to Opton's own, "I mean you go over there and the rules are completely different. You kill people and you see people you love get killed. You see horrible things and do horrible things and have horrible things done to you, and then you come back to this nice civilized life and you pause…How do you come to terms with it?" (Nagy and Stocke 2012). The photographs of Davenport and Opton both invite "the public to see the impact of war on a young person's face" (Nagy and Stocke 2012). For Opton, the impact reflected is of direct experience. For Davenport, the impact captured is from deferred experience: the experience of living in a society constructed within the visual economies of war as well as the experience of reconstructing a world in which individuals and communities seek to craft and control their own encounter with historical reality.

An important aspect of this performance of identity-construction and the perpetual crafting of reality is repetition. For Davenport, repetition is highlighted in the layering of enactments and re-enactments performed by her subjects, her camera, and her performances. Opton uses repetition in each of her series of soldiers and veterans as a framing device: the images all share the same staging, props, and technical aspect—only the faces themselves change. Similarity and difference are emphasized by the repetitions, as is the constructedness of the form. Wafaa Bilal uses repetition to extreme effect in 2007's "Domestic Tension," a deeply provocative, interactive performance piece.[7] For a month-long period, Bilal confined himself to a tiny space in a gallery, trapped in front of a camera and a remote-controlled paintball gun. Visitors to the gallery and Internet viewers watching online could activate the paintball gun, shooting Bilal at will, 24 hours a day. Born in Iraq but living and working in America, Bilal challenges his viewers—art gallery patrons and Internet masses alike—to "shoot an Iraqi." For 31 days and nights, video cameras captured Bilal as he was pelted by paint, engaged with viewers on YouTube and via chat rooms, struggling to maintain his composure, and at points, apparently, his sanity. Bilal's narration of his experience is barely intelligible over the repeated, obnoxiously loud gun blasts. Bilal combines performance, video voyeurism, audience participation, and direct communication to draw the viewer into the production and performance of his piece, baiting his audience, implicating his viewer, and educating with the exchange. Challenging the viewer to recognize all that makes the faraway Iraqi war seem unreal to an American, Bilal's website states his objective:

> ...to keep in mind the relationship of the viewer to the artwork... to transform the normally passive experience of viewing art into an active participation... to raise awareness of virtual war and privacy, or lack thereof, in the digital age.
>
> (Bilal "Domestic")

Like Davenport, then, Bilal explores the relationships between the virtual and the real in the language of art and violence. Unlike Davenport, however, Bilal emphasizes the dichotomy between the two, drawing attention to the material reality of human conditions and the potentially unseen consequences of virtual action. Having lost his brother to an unmanned

American drone, Bilal questions the awareness of the multi-media gamers who celebrate both worlds without distinction. Bilal engages directly with the ethics and politics of visual economy, joining Butler in witnessing the "precariousness" of life and recognizing the "ways in which visual and discursive fields are part of war recruitment and war waging" (Butler 2010: ix). Bilal's work is directly critical and oppositional, unlike the more abstracted work of Opton and open-ended work of Davenport. They share a challenge, not directly to war, but to its unseen visual economies and its repetition of frames. As Bilal explains, in the face of irremediable war, "It is our duty as artists and citizens to improvise strategies of engagement for dialogue… to create alternative narratives and perspectives" (Bilal "Virtual").

All three artists critique the power of the visual machine of war and challenge desensitization, disconnection, and disengagement. Rather than documenting the suffering of others for the visual consumption of the comfortable, each constructs a platform on which viewers are provoked to conceive of trauma, to reflect on conflict and in the construction of self. For Bilal and Davenport, the realms of gaming and virtuality are ripe for this interrogation: "The game holds up a mirror that reveals our own propensities for violence, racism and propaganda" (Bilal "Virtual"). In his broader challenge to the humanist philosophy of experience, Ian Bogost points to the crucial role of performance and reception in an augmented world. He argues that the computer is a machine that pretends to be other machines, working to "*simulate* any other machine by carrying out its logic through programmed instructions" (Bogost 2012). A society whose reality is augmented by the computer is one in which, "*intelligence*—whatever it is, the thing that goes on inside a human or a machine—is less interesting and productive a topic of conversation than the *effects* of such a process, the experience it creates in observers and interlocutors." This "pretense," he explains, is one of the theater. Just as we would not confuse the actor with the performance, Bogost argues, we must not reduce the effects of our experience to the logic by and through which events are performed. Thus, the politics of complex visual economies do not override the affective import of the "expressive possibility space" of media forms (Bogost 2007). Furthermore, though not yet as well explored as media like photography, videogames hold the potential of political speech: "Games are an excellent medium for exploring complex problems like healthcare or war or taxation, and can manage it in a way that does such issues justice. It is also a great way to live in someone else's shoes— the store worker just as much as the space marine." As expressive possibilities, Davenport's mixed media encounters with wargamers engage the visceral forces of affect. Thus in the words of affect theorists Gregory J. Seigworth and Melissa Gregg, the work might "drive us toward movement, toward thought" (Seigworth 2010: 1) while directly responding to the issues of morale—in the "military and security geographies" of Ben Anderson (2012), but also in the psychic geographies of a trauma-savvy citizenry.

IV

Some Airsoft event companies are stereotypically bombastic about spectacle and dismissive of the cost of war. The Kill House, an event put on by a company named Knock Knock Productions, boasts of being "a sensory stimulating conglomoration [sic] of target arrays, blaring war ambience, visual distractions like smoke and strobe, a wide variety of target engagements, Trip [sic] wires, Custom [sic] theme scenarios… like: hostage rescue, plant the bomb, and assassination… Those of you with heart conditions may want to opt-out of this one. Game on!" ("Airsoft Kill House" 2006 and "Kill House" 2006). Such games may well court the spectacle that, in Debord's formulation:

> …obliterates the boundaries between self and world by crushing the self besieged by the presence-absence of the world. It also obliterates the boundaries between true and false by repressing all directly lived truth beneath the *real presence* of the falsehood maintained by the organization of appearances. Individuals who passively accept their subjection to an alien everyday reality are thus driven toward a madness that reacts to this fate by resorting to illusory magical techniques. The essence of this pseudoresponse to an unanswerable communication is the acceptance and consumption of commodities. The consumer's compulsion to imitate is a truly infantile need, conditioned by all the aspects of his fundamental dispossession.
>
> (Debord 1967: 219)

When Davenport encounters actual players, however, the bombast gives way to more interesting performances of identity-formation. As Opton explains, "It is not sensationalism I am after. I am after the human being." Like Opton and Bilal, Davenport shoots with an eye to the ethical stakes of the making and deployment of images. As bearer of witness to events, images function in a complex politics. For these artists, a reinvigorated politics of visibility may provide a redemptive response to war. The imagined encounters of virtual reality can augment the exploration that is identity-formation for individuals, sub-communities, and national psyches.

One of Davenport's gamers explains, "'two is one, one is none'… by yourself you are worthless, doesn't matter who is better or more skilled." The augmented self-imagined in *Theater of*

War uses the traumatic latency in experience to authorize a new reality, one that allows for communal acceptance. This augmented self might redefine the horror of trauma by restructuring subjective encounter with experience on the free play recognized in inherent latency—not evacuate the horror, but redeploy it in a new visual economy that recognizes the choice of augmented encounter. As the gamers change the discourse from the search for "authentic" experience to one of "augmented" experience, the focus changes from individual visual experiences to the means of linking, sorting, and organizing them. Perhaps here, in the poetics of an augmented reality, we might find the potential for revolution described by Debord and the *Situationist International* in 1963: "Rediscovering poetry may merge with reinventing revolution… The point is not to put poetry at the service of revolution, but to put revolution at the service of poetry…The same judgment leads us to announce the total disappearance of poetry in the old forms in which it was produced and consumed and to announce its return in effective and unexpected forms. Our era no longer has to *write poetic directives;* it has to carry them out" ("All the King's Men"). In the poetics of gaming, it is the potential to "respawn": to be recreated as a new entity after its destruction. What Davenport's work calls for is a respawning of the augmented self, one unhindered by the digital divide and ready to encounter events with the political potential of free play inherent in experience. •

REFERENCES

"About the Angel Team." March 18, 2011. *YouTube.* [video online] Available at http://www.youtube.com/watch?v=nS2g_9mbQYE [Accessed July 10, 2012].

"Airsoft Evike.com—Lion claws X action footage." June 28, 2011. *YouTube.* [video online] Available at http://www.youtube.com/watch?v=VqbWXIUmBUY [Accessed June 23, 2012].

"Airsoft Kill House Fresno Calif." October 17, 2006. *MilitaryPhotos.Net.* Available at http://www.militaryphotos.net/forums/showthread.php?94407-Airsoft-Kill-House-Fresno-Calif [Accessed June 2, 2012].

Anderson, Ben. April 2010. "Morale and the affective geographies of the 'War on Terror.'" In *Cultural Geographies.* Vol. 17, # 2, pp. 219–236.

Baer, Ulrich. 2002. *Spectral Evidence: The Photography of Trauma.* Cambridge, Massachusetts: MIT Press.

Battlesim. Battlesim.com LLC. 2002–2012. Available at http://www.battlesim.com/different.html [Accessed July 2, 2012].

Baudrillard, Jean. 1995. *Simulacra and Simulation* (trans. Sheila Faria Glaser). University of Michigan Press.

Bilal, Wafaa. 2008. *Shoot an Iraqi: Art, Life and Resistance Under the Gun*. San Francisco: City Lights Publishers.

Bilal, Wafaa. "Domestic tension." *WafaaBilal.com*. Available at http://wafaabilal.com/domestic-tension/ [Accessed May 2, 2012].

Bilal, Wafaa. "Virtual jihadi." *WafaaBilal.com*. Available at http://wafaabilal.com/virtual-jihadi/ [Accessed May 2, 2012].

Bogost, Ian. July 16, 2012. "The great pretender: Turing as a philosopher of imitation." *The Atlantic*. The Atlantic Monthly Group. Available at http://www.theatlantic.com/technology/archive/2012/07/the-great-pretender-turing-as-a-philosopher-of-imitation/259824/# [Accessed May 2, 2012].

Bogost, Ian. August 8, 2007. "Time for Games to Grow Up." *The Guardian*. Available at http://www.guardian.co.uk/technology/2007/aug/08/comment.games [Accessed May 2, 2012].

Bulajewski, Mike. February 3, 2012. "There is only cyberspace." *Mr. Teacup*. Available at http://www.mrteacup.org/post/there-is-only-cyberspace.html [Accessed May 2, 2012].

Butler, Judith. 2010. *Frames of War*. New York: Verso.

Butler, Judith. 1999. *Gender Trouble*. New York: Routledge.

Carey, James W. 2008. *Communication as Culture: Essays on Media and Society*. New York: Routledge.

Caruth, Cathy. 1995. *Trauma: Explorations in Memory*. Baltimore: Johns Hopkins University Press.

Casper, Jim. 2008. "Soldier: A series of portraits by Suzanne Opton." *Lens Culture*. Available at http://www.lensculture.com/opton.html [Accessed May 2, 2012].

Davenport, Meredith. *Theater of War*. Available at www.meredithdavenport.com/theater-of-war [Accessed May 10, 2012].

Davenport, Meredith. March 2005. "Medellin stories from an urban war." *National Geographic*, p. 72.

Davenport, Meredith. 2012. "The New Venezuela." *National Geographic Society*. Available at http://ngm.nationalgeographic.com/2006/04/new-venezuela/davenport-photography [Accessed June 1, 2012].

Davenport, Meredith. January 23, 2005. "The next Islamist revolution?" *The New York Times Magazine*, p. 35.

Debord, Guy. 2005. *Society of the Spectacle*, 1967 (trans. Ken Knabb, February 2002). London: Rebel Press.

Debord, Guy and The Situationist International. 2006. "All the kings men" 1963. *Situationist*

International Anthology (trans. Ken Knabb). Oakland, CA: Bureau of Public Secrets.

Flusser, Vilém. 2000. Towards a Philosophy of Photography. London: Reaktion.

Foucault, Michel. 1995. *Discipline and Punish*. New York: Vintage.

Freud, Sigmund. 1947. *Moses and Monotheism* (trans. Katherine Jones). New York: Knopf.

---. 1896. "The Aetiology of Hysteria." In James Strachey (ed.), *The Standard Edition of the Complete Psychological Works of Sigmund Freud*. London: Hogarth Press, pp. 191–221.

Jurgenson, Nathan. October 26, 2010. "About cyborgology." In Nathan Jurgenson and PJ Rey (eds), *Cyborgology*. Available at http://thesocietypages.org/cyborgology/about/ [Accessed November 30, 2011].

"Kill house." October 12, 2006. Knock Knock Productions. *YouTube*. Available at http://www.youtube.com/watch?v=TnzM4ARLUb0 [Accessed July 12, 2012].

Levy, Michael S. July, 1998. "A helpful way to conceptualize and understand re-enactments." *Journal of Psychotherapy Practice and Research*. American Psychiatric Press, Inc. Vol. 7, pp. 227–235.

Leys, Ruth. 2000. *Trauma: A Genealogy*. Chicago: University of Chicago Press.

Lieberman, Jessica. March, 2008. "Traumatic images." *Photographies*. Vol. 1, No. 1.

Participant 6. January 7, 2007. Unpublished Interview. Interviewed by Meredith Davenport [video]. Culpeper, Virginia.

Lion Claws. 2012. Operation Lion Claws Military Simulation Series. Available at http://www.oplionclaws.com/ [Accessed June 16, 2012].

MindGame Productions. 2011. MindGame Productions. http://www.mindgame-productions.com/ [Accessed June 16, 2012].

Moakley, Paul. November 23, 2011. "Soldier down: The portraits of Suzanne Opton." *Time Light Box*. Available at http://lightbox.time.com/2011/11/23/soldier-down-the-portraits-of-suzanne-opton/#1 [Accessed July 12, 2012].

Mukherjee, Souvik and Pitchford, Jenna. 2010. "'Shall we kill the pixel soldier?': perceptions of trauma and morality in combat video games." *Journal of Gaming and Virtual Worlds*. Vol. 2. No. 1.

Nagy, Kimberly and Stocke, Joy. July, 2012. "Art-interview Suzanne Opton and Michael Fay: The human face of war." *Wild River Review*. Available at http://www.wildriverreview.com/interview/art/suzanne-opton-michael-fay/human-faces-of-war/kim%20Nagy/Joy-E-Stocke [Accessed July 12, 2012].

Opton, Suzanne. "Soldier." *Suzanneopton.com*. Available at http://suzanneopton.com/#/soldier [Accessed May 12, 2012].

Opton, Suzanne. 2011. *Suzanne Opton: Soldier, many wars*. Seattle: Decode Books.

"'Paintball terrorists' convicted of conspiracy." March 2004. FOX News Network, LLC. Available at http://www.foxnews.com/story/0,2933,113310,00.html [Accessed May 12, 2012].

Participant 1. December 31, 2006. Unpublished Interview. Interviewed by Meredith Davenport [video]. Tacoma Washington.

Participant 3. December 31, 2006. Unpublished Interview. Interviewed by Meredith Davenport [video]. Tacoma, Washington.

Participant 4. November 19, 2006. Unpublished Interview. Interviewed by Meredith Davenport [video]. Fresno, California.

Participant 6. January 7, 2007. Unpublished Interview. Interviewed by Meredith Davenport [video]. Culpeper, Virginia.

Participant 7. January 20, 2007. Unpublished Interview. Interviewed by Meredith Davenport [video]. Ocala, Florida.

"PTSD: A growing epidemic." Winter 2009. *NIH Medline Plus*. Vol. 4, No. 1, pp. 10–14. Available at http://www.nlm.nih.gov/medlineplus/magazine/issues/winter09/articles/winter09pg10-14.html [Accessed December 12, 2011].

Rey, PJ. February 1, 2012. "There is no 'cyberspace.'" In Nathan Jurgenson and PJ Rey (eds), *Cyborgology*. Available at http://thesocietypages.org/cyborgology/2012/02/01/there-is-no-cyberspace/ [Accessed February 12, 2012].

Seigworth, Gregory J. and Melissa Gregg. 2010. "An inventory of shimmers." *The Affect Theory Reader*. Durham: Duke University Press.

Sontag, Susan. 1990. *On Photography*. 1st Anchor Books ed. New York: Anchor Books.

"Study: Rates of PTSD among Afghanistan, Iraq soldiers dramatically lower than predicted." May 17, 2012. *Psychology & Psychiatry*. Available at http://medicalxpress.com/news/2012-05-ptsd-afghanistan-iraq-soldiers.html [Accessed December 12, 2011].

Tufekci, Zeynep. February 8, 2012. "Breaking bread, breaking digital dualism." *Technosociology: Our Tools, Ourselves*. Available at http://technosociology.org/?p=747 [Accessed May 12, 2011].

"What makes us different?" Battlesim.com LLC. 2002–2012. Available at http://www.battlesim.com/different.html [Accessed June 12, 2011].

Wiener, Norbert. (1948) 1965. *Cybernetics: Or Control and Communication in the Animal and the Machine*. Cambridge, Massachusetts: MIT Press.

Zoroya, Gregg. November 30, 2011. "Rise in PTSD cases from two wars strains resources." *USA Today*. Available at http://www.usatoday.com/news/military/story/2011-11-29/PTSD-cases-rise/51476604/1. [Accessed December 12, 2011].

ENDNOTES

1   See the work of journalists such as David Carr and scholars such as Sherry Turkle, Zeynep Tufekci and James W Carey as well as the ideas of Norbert Wiener.

2   MindGame Productions claims to be the "longest running Airsoft-events company on the east coast." Established in 2005, it is based in Florida "with team members spread through Florida, Georgia, Virginia, Pennsylvania, Ohio, and Texas." The website explains that events, "run the gamut from intense, military simulation events to immersive and stimulating games drawing from science fiction and alternate history themes. MGP hosts events at military and law-enforcement training facilities, scenario paintball fields, empty warehouse, and office buildings" (MindGame 2011). Battlesim.com LLC advertises to "gaming communities and gaming players with a primary focus on 'war' or 'battle' simulations… [which] range from Airsoft events to PC gaming." Their immersive environments are highly orchestrated: "Units are given an overview and warning order for their missions and encouraged to formulate a plan, rehearse that plan, and execute it during a simulated mission phase. Following virtually every mission they are debriefed and coached by skilled and knowledgeable cadre. Our approach requires planning, organization and support as well as expertise, props, and setup" (Battlesim 2002–2012).

3   Most of the laws concern the danger of realistic-looking guns. But there have also been cases that involve gaming itself as a potential crime. In 2004, for example, three Americans were convicted of conspiracy charges for "using paintball games to train for holy war" (Fox News 2004).

4   Some videos place first-person-shooter viewpoint footage into other forms of aerial or third-person viewpoint footage, for multiple aspect video experiences. See, for example, some of the frame-within-a-frame work with Lion Claws ("Airsoft Evike.com" 2011).

5   "Soldier" enjoyed a subsequent print publication with the "Many Wars" series in *Suzanne Opton: Soldier/Many Wars* in 2011. "Many Wars" focuses on veterans of Iraq and Afghanistan as well as those of World War II, the cold war, and Vietnam.

6   The "Many Wars" series continues this larger conceptual project, moving on to veterans who are now "seeking treatment for combat trauma that is either very fresh or has haunted them for a lifetime" (http://suzanneopton.com/#/veterans).

7   Bilal details his experience in the book *Shoot an Iraqi: Art, Life and Resistance Under the Gun* (2008).